VOODOO AND POLITICS IN HAITI

Voodoo and Politics in Haiti

Michel S. Laguerre

Associate Professor of Caribbean Affairs
University of California at Berkeley

St. Martin's Press   New York

First published in the United States of America in 1989

Printed in Hong Kong

ISBN 0–312–02066–X

Library of Congress Cataloging-in-Publication Data
Laguerre, Michel S.
Voodoo and politics in Haiti.
Bibliography: p.
Includes index.
1. Voodooism—Haiti.   2. Religion and politics—
Haiti.   3. Haiti—Religion.   4. Haiti—Politics and
government.   I. Title.
BL2490.L26   1989   299'.67   88–18181
ISBN 0–312–02066–X

To Joujou, Lily and Agathe

Contents

List of Illustrations

Introduction

This book, which explains the intricate relationship between Voodoo and politics in Haiti from the colonial period to the present, is part of my ongoing research into the functioning of Caribbean political and urban institutions. When the country achieved its independence in 1804, the majority of its political leaders and army officers and soldiers were still Voodoo practitioners. Although the first constitution proclaimed the Catholic church the official church of the new republic, it remains true that the Voodoo faith could not and did not evaporate overnight, partly because of the strategic, religious and ideological role it played during the Haitian revolution. Voodoo is found to be an ingredient of some weight in the nascent formation and development of post-independence Haitian political process. The itinerary or trajectory of this functional but informal marriage between Voodoo and politics is here expounded.

Ever since the colonial era, the Voodoo church has been an underground political institution in Haiti and the Voodoo priest a political middleman. In fact, the active participation of Voodoo leaders in the Haitian revolution was of critical importance to the early independence of the colony in 1804. On 14 August 1791, a slave and Voodoo priest named Boukman organised a mammoth Voodoo ceremony on one of the northern plantations. During a possession trance, he informed his brethren and associates that the Voodoo spirits wanted their help in eliminating the French from the colony and liberating the slaves. The slave rebellion that followed was headed by several Voodoo priests and maroon – fugitive slave – leaders in various parts of the colony.

After independence, in order to protect their freedom and their land, former slaves and maroons congregated in secret societies around influential Voodoo priests. Throughout the nineteenth century they participated in and organised peasant revolts against the appropriation of their land by influential politicians and army officers. One must also add that they served at times as back-up paramilitary units to the regular army when the country was in a state of alert – both to resist an imminent foreign invasion, and to undertake the invasions of the Dominican Republic. During the US occupation, 1915–34, their existence was made known through their participation in the 'Kako' resistance movement. They launched large-scale guerilla

1

warfare against the marines and even after their heroic leaders were killed did not disappear from the scene but simply retreated to their home communities.

During the presidential elections of 1957, there were half a dozen secret societies that had almost complete control over the daily life of the Haitian peasantry and urban dwellers. As a kind of underground police force, judicial body and regional government, they issued their members with passports that have ever since been honoured as a diplomatic instrument by local branches of their organisation in various hamlets, villages and cities throughout the country.

Presidential candidate François Duvalier was able to identify and exploit intelligently these networks of relationships to the extent that some Voodoo priests openly used their temples as local headquarters for his campaign. Later, when Duvalier was elected president, he invited a few Voodoo priests and secret society leaders to serve as his special assistants and advisors. When he decided to form the Tonton Macoute force of civilian militiamen, members of the secret societies and Voodoo churches were recruited to serve along with other militiamen. Until recently, several Tonton Macoute units who played a role in national security were headed by notorious Voodoo priests.

Unlike his father, Jean-Claude Duvalier gave the impression of distancing himself from most of the Voodoo and secret society leaders. As a consequence in the weeks prior to the collapse of his administration, a group of Voodoo priests and priestesses made it clear to the president that they could no longer support him – I was actually informed by one of the Voodoo priests that a letter had been circulated amongst them telling them to withhold their support from the regime. The content of the letter was passed on to the president by an influential Voodoo priest in Port-au-Prince, the *porte-parole* of the group.

While the Port-au-Prince Voodoo priests were advising the president on the best course of action to take, others in the Artibonite Valley – especially in the city of Gonaives and the town of Saint Marc – were actively engaged in the *Déchoukaj* (Uproot) Operation and openly participated in protests against his administration. The empty coffin seen carried on the heads of two protesters with the sign 'Jean-Claude Duvalier, you belong there' was an indication that a secret society wanted to punish him after he had been found guilty by the council of elders. He was seen as having betrayed the promises made by his own father in courting the local bourgeoisie at the expense of the black masses.

In the minds of many Haitians, François and Jean-Claude Duvalier were able to remain for so long in office because of the support of the Tontons Macoutes, many of them Voodoo leaders in their own communities. After Jean-Claude Duvalier left Port-au-Prince on 7 February 1986, on board a US Air Force C-141 military plane en route to temporary exile in France, several Voodoo priests went underground – prompted by their close association with the fallen regime – while others were harassed, beaten up or lynched by urban and rural mobs throughout the country. The most hated and persecuted Voodoo priests were members of the Tonton Macoute force – notorious for its human rights abuses.

Opération Déchoukaj – and later on to a certain extent *Opération Raché Manyok* (grub up weeds) and *Opération Balérousé* (clear the land) – was not intended to be a persecution of the Voodoo church *per se*, but of identifiable Voodoo priests because of their past abuse of power. In fact not every Voodoo priest was persecuted, but only those who were seen as political exploiters and who had had some dealings with the Duvalier administration. In such a politically motivated operation, no doubt mistakes were made. It was later found by the Director of the Bureau of Ethnology that a handful of those lynched were victims of mistaken identity. The Voodoo priests who suffered the most – we were told by our informants – were those who operated relatively speaking alone, or those who were protected by a weak entourage – those secret society members who were supposed to defend the congregation and its leaders.

Despite the persecution of some of its members, the Voodoo church is still alive and well in Haiti during the post-Duvalier era. During the summer of 1986, while I was conducting a public opinion poll in Haiti to identify the front-runners among the presidential candidates (Michel S. Laguerre, *Electoral Politics in Haiti: A Public Opinion Poll*. Berkeley: Institute for the Study of Social Change, University of California at Berkeley, 1987), I became aware that one of them owned a Voodoo temple. Another influential candidate had strong Voodoo connections and was holder of a secret society passport. Whichever way an analyst looks at it, Voodoo still remains today an ingredient of some weight and importance in the Haitian electoral and political process.

To shed light on the relations between Voodoo and politics a few topics were selected for critical investigation. Chapter 1 discusses the liberating, integrative and repressive roles of Voodoo in Haitian society. It elaborates on the historical, political and structural reasons why Voodoo – which arose as a messianic movement during the Haitian revolution – became after independence a functional force for the maintenance of the status quo and why it was transformed during the Duvalier era into a force of repression. The relations of Voodoo adherents to other influential sectors of Haitian society are also analysed.

Chapter 2 analyses the development of Voodoo from a household based ritual to an extended family based ritual and finally to a public church. The evolution of colonial Voodoo is seen as related to the transformation in the political economy and the shifts in the demographic structures of the colony.

Chapter 3 focuses on the maroon situation in colonial Haiti and specifically the practice of Voodoo among urban, nomadic and rural maroons. They are seen as having their own brand of Voodoo – in many respects different from, but at the same time having some similar features to that practised in the plantations. The maroons are believed to be the precursors of the secret societies of today.

Chapter 4 documents the messianic role of Voodoo during the colonial era and the heroic participation of Voodoo leaders during the Haitian revolution. The successful outcome of the wars of independence was in part due to those urban and rural *guerilleros* who, through their tactical manoeuvers, were able to keep a military pressure on the French colonial administration which finally led them to defeat. Placing their faith in their Voodoo spirit protectors, the leaders fought the French with great ferocity until the ultimate victory.

Chapter 5 presents a functional analysis of the Bizango secret society. Its *modus operandi* is described and the reasons for its existence are explained. The Bizango secret society is seen as a post-independence outgrowth of pre-independence maroon organisations. Its role as a paramilitary force is also spelled out.

The importance of the shrine of Saut D'Eau as a centre of Voodoo and Christian pilgrimage is presented in Chapter 6. This chapter also documents how politicians have been using Saut D'Eau to advance their own causes and to incite Haitian soldiers to fight – in the nineteenth century against the Dominican army and early this century against the US marines.

Chapter 7 focuses on the Duvalier regime and its use of Voodoo. It delineates how the local Voodoo churches are structurally linked to the national structure of Haitian politics. It shows that both the Duvalier administrations and the Voodoo leaders gained from the exploitation of Voodoo in local and national politics. From being a liberating force Voodoo had become an oppressive institution. The circumstances that allowed this to happen are also delineated.

Finally, in Chapter 8, the military symbolism in Voodoo as well as the organisation of Voodoo territorial, mystical and ritual space is discussed. Although the post-Duvalierian Haitian Constitution of 1987 revoked in its Article 297a the decree of 5 September 1935, against superstitious beliefs, it falls short of providing a legal status to Voodoo. The chapter explains the policies of the state *vis-à-vis* Voodoo from the colonial era onwards and discusses how the Haitian parliament may go about developing a comprehensive policy toward the Voodoo church.

Some portions of the book have been read at faculty seminars and at national and international scholarly meetings. Chapter 1 was read at the International Conference on 'Haiti: A Nation in Transition' sponsored by Sethon Hall University, financed by the New Jersey Department of Higher Education and the New Jersey Committee for the Humanities and held 1–3 May, 1987. Chapter 2 was delivered as a public lecture at the Graduate Theological Union at Berkeley, 14 February 1977. Chapter 3 was presented at the IXth International Congress of Ethnological and Anthropological Sciences, Chicago, 5 September 1973. Chapter 4 was read at a scholarly meeting organised by the Martin Luther King, Jr Program in Black Churches Studies at Colgate Rochester Divinity School and held in Haiti 21–28 January 1974. Chapter 7 was read at an International Conference on 'New Perspectives on Caribbean Studies: Toward the 21st Century,' sponsored by the Research Institute for the Study of Man, financed by the National Science Foundation and held at Hunter College, the City University of New York, 29 August 1984. And finally Chapter 8 was delivered at an International Conference on 'African Religions: Creativity, Imagination and Expressions' organised by the Divinity School of Howard University, and held 10–12 December 1986.

Some chapters have been previously published elsewhere. We have revised, adapted and in some cases enlarged them. For example, Chapter 2 appeared in *Journal of the Interdenominational Theological Centre* 5 (Fall): 47–60, 1977. Chapter 4 was published in *Freeing the Spirit* Vol. III, No. 1, pp. 23–28, 1974. Chapter 5 was a contribution to *Secrecy: A Cross-cultural Perspective* edited by Stanton Tefft, New York: Human Sciences Press, pp. 147–160, 1980. Chapter 6 was published in *Social Campass: International Review of Sociology of Religion*, Vol. 23, No. 1, pp. 5–21, 1986. Chapter 7 appeared in a French version under the title 'Politique et Vaudou en Haiti: L'Ere des Duvalier 1957–1986,' in *Collectif Paroles*, No. 33, pp. 41–48, 1987. Finally a summary of the book was commissioned by *The Wall Street Journal* and published in the American edition of 18 April 1986, and in the British edition of 22 April 1986.

I am grateful to all who participated in these academic meetings, questioned my assumptions and provided me with the impetus to rethink the issues. I am particularly thankful to Regina Holloman and Norman E. Whitten, Jr who generously read early drafts of Chapter 2, 3 and 4 while I was still in the process of familiarising myself with the grammatical peculiarities and the idiomatic contours of the English language. I also wish to give thanks to Max Blanchet and Linh Do for drawing the figures and to my secretary Elmirie Robinson-Cephas for diligently typing the manuscript. Finally I am grateful to the Committee on Research of the University of California at Berkeley for awarding me a Faculty grant to undertake the preparation of the manuscript for publication.

1 Religion and Politics

Although Voodoo may mean different things to different people, the mass media have apparently agreed to identify the republic of Haiti as the land of Voodoo *par excellence* in the western hemisphere. Several historically identifiable events and circumstances – not least the sensationalist international press reportage and various reports and books by foreign dignitaries in mission in Port-au-Prince – have bestowed that notorious reputation on the old republic. As one reads nineteenth-century accounts by foreigners, one encounters bizarre Voodoo practices, nonsensical beliefs and engrossing stories of zombification and cannibalism.[1] These reports tended to exaggerate in order to make the stories more exciting, and their emphasis is on exotic rituals and concomitant, supposedly criminal, practices.

To the student of Haitian politics, Voodoo cannot simply be reduced to a bunch of mumbo-jumbo rituals. It is a fundamental factor in the rapport of forces in Haiti because it helps shape the structure of relationships between the various sectors of society.

To my knowledge, the political dimension of Voodoo has not yet been studied systematically in all its ramifications. This study – in focusing on the relationship between Voodoo and politics – hopes to fill that void. Historically, the Voodoo church developed as a reaction of the oppressed slaves to the religious and political domination of their colonial oppressors. Throughout the nineteenth and twentieth centuries, state domestic politics and policies have affected the organisation of the Voodoo church, which, in turn, has also infiltrated the matrix of local and national level politics. As political and historical circumstances evolved, Voodoo also underwent changes in its religious ideology, ritual practices and modes of interaction with the state apparatus. Thus the politics of Voodoo has so far been one of reactions and responses to structural constraints generated in the wider society.

In the seventeenth and eighteenth centuries, under the peculiar system of slavery, a nativistic movement composed mostly of Voodoo believers developed in French colonial Haiti.[2] This mass movement evolved in an effort to achieve political, religious and cultural freedom from metropolitan France. As the slaves could not use institutional state mechanisms to publicise their case against the cruelty of slavery, Voodoo became one of the main channels they appropriated to fight the colonial system. In an effort to shed light on the relationship between Voodoo and politics. I shall identify the different variables that explain the formation and the success of this slave movement.

Although it is possible to make certain general theoretical statements about the relationship between religion and other aspects of socio-cultural organisation, each historical situation is, to a certain extent, unique in its configuration of variables. In the case of Haiti, this unique configuration explains, first, why Haitian religion took a nativist form, second, why it took a mainly political rather than an escapist form, and, third, why it (alone among New World nativist movements) was successful. I see these variables as being the following:

1. The plantation system, which set the pattern both of spatial and social-structural relations within the population.
2. The black demographic revolution, itself related to the particular political economy of the island.
3. The phenomenon of *marronage*, that is, the development by former slaves of separate communities outside the framework of the plantation system.

Voodoo developed as a politico-religious phenomenon rather than as a strictly religious or psycho-religious phenomenon (which, under other historical-processual circumstances, it might have done) in active opposition to politico-economic domination from metropolitan France and under the conditions previously cited. Voodoo became a successful channel used by both maroons and slaves to express their resistance to the colonial regime.

The French colony of Haiti was not one of 'settlement,' but rather one of 'exploitation' (Best 1968: 286). By that it is meant that the colonists were not interested in staying on the island for life, but only in amassing enough money to return to live in France.[3] The colony was characterised by an economy based on the plantation system, field work done by African and Creole slaves, and by colonial status as an overseas extension of the metropolitan economy. Furthermore, in this colonial society, the economy was managed by a minority of whites seeking their own benefits and those of the European metropolis. Yet, over the passage of time, the society developed a separate and unique cultural identity; its inhabitants were acculturated to one another and to the emerging Creole culture.

The course of French colonial Haiti's development as a separate cultural-social unit can be divided into three periods, contrasting in terms of the size and composition of the population, the gross earnings of the economy and the structure of the social system as a whole. They are:

1. The pre-sugar plantation period (1625–97).
2. The period of intense exploitation of the land (1698–1791).
3. The period of decline (1791–1803).

These periods are characterised by a certain number of specific features that differentiate between them. The pre-sugar plantation period is roughly characterised by a diversity of small property holdings (Redsons 1970: 13). During this period, the population was divided into European colonists, African slaves and Amerindians. People of African descent comprised a small group both numerically and socially.[4] Maroon camps, located in only a few places, were not yet a danger to the well-being of the colony (Fouchard 1953: 17). Periodic slave revolts were short-lived and did not have a noticeably negative effect on the general policy of the colonial government and the day-to-day life of the colonists, while Voodoo as a Creole cult was in its inception and developed basically as a household-based ritual (Denis and Duvalier 1944: 5).

The period of intense exploitation of the land, which reveals considerable changes in economic and demographic parameters, coincides with the sugar revolution (1698–1791). It is marked by the passage from small to large property holdings and the beginning of a demographic revolution during which the white population was literally 'swamped' by the rapid increase in the number of slaves and free blacks.[5] The population was divided into three distinct social classes: the whites, the slaves and the freedmen. The number of Indians still living in the colony was negligible. The economy became one of highly controlled exchange, the products of the colony being exchanged for those of the metropolis (Redsons 1970: 17). In order to survive in the hostile plantation milieu, black families developed such strategies as strong kinship bonds (Trouillot 1957: 27; Dutertre 1667: 518; Labat 1742, IV: 186), strong work orientation (Bellegarde 1953: 45), adaptability of family roles (Bellegarde 1953: 46–67) and strong religious orientation (Debien 1967: 525–555. See also Hill 1971). Fugitive slaves, organised in maroon settlements all over the island (Debien 1966: 20), launched several raids on neighbouring plantations. Administrators, colonists and the clergy at times took strong measures to eradicate the emerging Creolised Afro-cults and maroon settlements from the colony. The Saturday night meetings –

when slaves in the darkness of the slave quarters danced *Calenda* and Voodoo – were outlawed but continued in secret and became contexts for raising the political consciousness of the slaves (Price-Mars 1928: 35). During those meetings, slaves became politically aware of their enslaved condition and looked for ways of overcoming their oppression.

The period of decline corresponds to the period of the revolutionary troubles (1791–1803), during which the black demographic revolution reached its peak while colonists were leaving the colony en masse. This period is singularly marked by the decline of the economy as slaves burned a large number of plantations in an effort to get rid of their masters (James 1963: 270–389). Voodoo, as practised in the maroon camps and on the plantations, underwent a cross-breeding. Maroon chiefs and Voodoo priests became leaders of the slave revolutionary movement using Voodoo as a political ideology to motivate the black population into revolt against the colonial system (Mennesson-Rigaud 1958: 62). Thus, with Voodoo as a unifying factor of social cohesion, the slaves fought hard to expel or eliminate their colonial masters and to lead the colony toward the path of national independence.

Any slave society in which the slaves greatly outnumber the colonists is ripe for revolution. However, in order to succeed, such a revolution may need one or more charismatic leaders who can attract a large number of followers. In the case of colonial Haiti, a nativistic movement organised and headed by Voodoo priests and maroon chiefs was born. Although social stratification occurred early in the period of intense exploitation of the land – laying the basis for developments in the eighteenth century and the period after independence – it was not the urban segment of the black-mulatto population that provided leadership in this early period. Rather, charismatic maroon leaders used the nativist religion as a channel for their political demands (Mennesson-Rigaud 1958: 64). Voodoo evolved as a politico-religious phenomenon and served, during the Haitian Revolution, as a vehicle for the expression of a separatist political ideology. However, throughout the nineteenth and twentieth centuries, Voodoo has played more of an integrative than a disruptive role in Haitian society.

INTEGRATIVE AND DISRUPTIVE ROLE OF RELIGION IN SOCIETY

Religion has been presented as having the capacity to play an integrative or disintegrative role in society. Indeed, according to a theoretical tradition running from Durkheim to Weber and Parsons, institutionalised religions are found to provide institutional mechanisms for integration. This functional approach to religion was first formulated by Durkheim, who, in *The Elementary Forms of the Religious Life* (1915), was mainly interested in developing a theory concerning the origins of religion, its role in primitive societies and its contribution to social integration. Contrary to Karl Marx, who saw religion as an epiphenomenon, 'the opiate of the people', Durkheim considered religion 'the source of all higher culture.' In fact, he argued that 'all the great social institutions have been born in religion' (Durkheim 1915: 418).

Furthermore, Durkheim conceived of society as divided into two spheres: the sacred and the profane. For him the sacred functions mainly to evoke awe and serves as the basis for societal values. Religion then appears as the institutionalisation of the sacred and plays a positive role in integrating society. In that same line of thinking, he noted that 'before all, rites are means by which the social group reaffirms itself periodically' (Durkheim 1915: 387).

Recalling Durkheim's and Malinowski's contributions to the functional significance of religion, Parsons (1949: 61) noted:

> It was Durkheim's view that religious ritual was of primary significance as a mechanism for expressing and reinforcing the sentiment most essential to the institutional integration of the society. It can readily be seen that this is clearly linked to Malinowski's views of the significance of funeral ceremonies as a mechanism for reasserting the solidarity of the group on the occasion of severe emotional strain. Thus Durkheim worked out certain aspects of the specific relations between religion and social structure more sharply than did Malinowski, and in addition put the problem in a different functional perspective in that he applied it to the society as a whole in abstraction for particular situations of tension and strain for the individual.

Like Durkheim, Max Weber showed in *The Protestant Ethic and the Spirit of Capitalism* (1930) the positive function of religion in the maintenance system of society. Weber demonstrated very well how the ethic of Protestantism and in particular the social ethic of Calvinism, has played an important role in the development of modern capitalism. However, he recognised that the Protestant ethic is only one cause among several.

Davis and Moore (1945: 244) also adhered to the notion of the integrative function of religion in society:

> The reason why religion is necessary is apparently to be found in the fact that human society achieves its unity primarily through the possession by its members of certain ultimate values and ends in common. Although these values and ends are subjective, they influence behaviour, and their integration enables this society to operate as a system.

I fully agree with Durkheim that the sacred and its institutionalisation can be used as solidarity mechanism. In fact, these may allow a large number of people to share similar values and to have a similar *weltanschauung*, thus integrating people into their society. However, the sacred can also, in situations of oppression, have a disruptive function. As Lanternari shows in *The Religions of the Oppressed* (1963), religion can also play a disruptive role in society. Lanternari is interested in analysing the causes that give birth to prophetic revitalisation and liberation movements. He discusses a wide range of such movements, including nativistic religious movements in Africa, prophetic movements in North America (among them the peyote cult), religious movements in Central and South America and messianic movements in Melanesia, Asia, Polynesia and Indonesia. His goal is basically to offer a 'history of religious movements among colonial and semi-colonial peoples' (Lanternari 1963: VIII). He concludes that although the official church had an integrative role in colonial societies, nativistic churches in these same societies sometimes had a disruptive function.

Nativistic movements include cargo cults, religious revivals, messianic movements, utopian movements, sect formations, mass movements, social movements and revolutionary and charismatic movements. These nativistic movements were born under various colonial and neo-colonial regimes, and according to Ralph Linton (1943: 230), they are 'any conscious, organised attempt on the part of a society's members to revive or perpetuate selected aspects of its culture'. Linton classifies these nativistic movements into two major types: revivalistic nativism and four minor types (magical revivalism, rational revivalism, magical perpetuation and rational perpetuation).

Even in recognising that the immediate causes of nativistic movements are highly variable, Linton (1943: 240) believes that they have 'as a common denominator a situation of inequality between the societies in contact. Such inequalities may derive either from the attitudes of the societies involved or from actual situations of dominance and submission'.

Looking at these movements from a psychological point of view, Wallace (1956) characterises them as 'revitalisation movements,' which he defines, refining Linton's definition, as 'any conscious, organised effort by members of a society to construct a more satisfying culture' (Wallace 1966: 30). Wallace (1966: 30) also points out the disruptive role these revitalisation movements played: 'Reformative religious movements far from being conservative, are often radically destructive of existing institutions, aiming to solve conflict not by manipulation of the self but by manipulation of the real world.'

Nativistic movements as a conscious phenomenon can be understood as a manifestation of ethnic pride and a consciousness of being exploited by a dominant sector of society. However, as Edmonson (1960: 185) remarks:

The existence of an ethnic self-conception would seem to be a necessary condition for the appearance of an ethnic nativistic movement. It is not a sufficient condition. The potential adherents of the cult must come to feel threatened in ethnic terms, and they must be convinced that there is hope in doing something about it.

Thus, nativistic movements can be interpreted as a form of resistance to both political subjugation and cultural domination. Lanternari (1963: 253) makes it clear that 'nativism is turned against western culture and aims to establish an exclusive cult for the natives, a new cult.' In *The Religions of the Oppressed*, he shows that native religions like Voodoo have played a very important political role in diverse geographical areas, for example, peyotism in America and kimbangu-ism in Bakongo. The Haitian revolutionary movement, centred upon Voodoo, was not the only example of nativist response to European colonisation of the New World – in other New World territories religious leaders also played a catalytic role in slave revolts. Thus, in the US South, a Christian prophet named Nat Turner believed that he had received from God the mission of liberating his unfortunate brothers (Aptheker 1968: 119). As a black preacher, Nat Turner made friends among his fellow slaves and organised an armed revolt against the slaveowners of the South. The revolt – which did not last long – failed on 21 August 1831, in Southampton County, Virginia, after the rebels had killed about 60 whites.

Runaway plantation slaves, many of the Muslim faith (Bastide 1961: 203), developed maroon communities in several areas of north-eastern Brazil. In fact, a great number of slave revolts recorded in Brazil between 1807 and 1835 were organised and managed by Muslims and 'fetishist' cult leaders whose identity was known to both the local whites and the slave population at large (Rodrigues 1932: 83; Bastide 1967: 53).

In Cuba, as in the other islands of the Caribbean, slaves gathered on Saturday evenings to perform social and religious dances and to worship their spirits. These meetings were forbidden by the colonial administration as soon as the colonists perceived their relationship to the periodic revolts of the plantation slaves.

> Formerly, it is said, might be heard every evening and night, both afar and near, the joyous sound of the African drum, as it was beaten at the Negro dances. When, however, it was discovered that these dancing assemblies had been made use of for the organisation of the disturbances which afterward took place, their liberty became very much circumscribed. (Bremer 1868: 346)

The secret societies that appeared in Trinidad during the colonial period were also headed by religious leaders. Often referred to as obeah-men and known as 'troublemakers,' these leaders were influential in organising the plot of 1808, whose goal was to kill 'all the whites' on the island. Fraser (1896, I: 269), who noted the existence of these secret societies, wrote:

> According to all witnesses, the slaves throughout the island but especially in Maraval, Diego Martin and Carenage (districts which were chiefly inhabited by French settlers), had formed themselves into 'Convois' and 'Regiments', each of which were known by its peculiar appellation . . .
>
> As these associations could not exist unnoticed, they had an avowed object harmless enough in a political sense though scarcely so from a moral point of view. They professed to meet merely for indulgence in those dances [of] which the African races are so inordinately fond. The witnesses stated probably the truth that by far the greater number of the members of these bands were kept in entire ignorance of their real object. If, however, the rest of their statements were correct, the chiefs had formed a diabolical

plot, which, had it not been most opportunely discovered, would have formed a terrible epoch in the history of the colony.

In Jamaica, maroon communities tried on various occasions to take over control of the colony. Here again, the obeah-men were known by the colonial power as slave leaders and the 'brains trusts' of periodic revolts. For that reason, white legislators of the island at times took strong, effective measures against them. When found guilty, the obeah-men were often sentenced to death or deportation (Brathwaite 1971: 162). Patterson (1967: 192), who has studied the mechanisms of resistance to slavery in Jamaica, writes about the role played by obeah in the slave revolts:

> Obeah functioned largely in the numerous rebellions of the slaves. This was particularly the case with the obeah-men from the Gold Coast, one of whom took a leading part in the serious uprising of 1760. In the plotting of these rebellions the obeah-man was essential in administering oaths of secrecy, and, in cases, distributing fetishes which were supposed to immunise the insurgents from the arms of the whites.

The slave preacher was sometimes instrumental in instilling the spirit of rebellion in the minds of his congregation. It was not by accident that in the middle of the maroon war in Jamaica, a black preacher, Moses Baker, read this verse from a Baptist hymn to the assembly:

> We will be slaves no more,
> Since Christ has made us free,
> Has nailed our tyrants to the cross,
> And bought our liberty.
> (Clark, Dendy, and Phillippo 1865: 34)

The preceding survey has shown various facets of the link between religion and politics in the Caribbean. In general, the church has practically never been a neutral or an apolitical institution. This can be seen in the history of the established churches planted in the colonies by the colonial powers to control and exploit the local populations. In Europe, during the period of the Crusades, the Catholic church was openly subservient to the dominant political powers. If in the case of the New World the state church was most often at the service of oppressors, there existed side by side examples where religion furthered a revolutionary ideology and fought on the side of the oppressed. Such was the case of Voodoo in colonial Haiti.

The slave revolts that exploded periodically in the Caribbean had at least two factors in common. The first is that most of the revolutionary leaders were also religious leaders. The second is that, for the most part, the revolts failed in their ultimate goal – that of eradicating the whites from the colonies. Some revolts were partially successful, especially those in Brazil and Surinam, to the degree that slaves took advantage of the uprisings to join autonomous maroon societies and develop alternative life-styles.

Like Voodoo, the nativistic religious movements previously cited were also foci for the growth of consciousness and for political fomentation. Without losing their religious impulse, these became radical movements of liberation with well-defined political goals. As Lanternari (1963: 3) points out: 'Premonitory religious movements of revival and transformation usually lie at the origin of every political or military uprising among the native peoples and take the form of messianic cults promising liberation'.

As a general rule, nativistic movements that emerge among oppressed people develop a political ideology focusing on the restoration of an era of freedom and the establishment of a better world. Their ideology is echoed in their search for freedom and salvation: 'Freedom from subjection and servitude to foreign powers as well as from adversity, and salvation from the possibility of having the traditional culture destroyed and the native society wiped out as a historical entity' (Lanternari 1963: 239).

According to Lanternari, the oppressed often conclude that the re-establishment of political autonomy is the key to the preservation of cultural autonomy. Unity of action arises from the fact that the diverse elements of the group agree on the seriousness of the threat to 'their way of life' and are motivated to co-operate in defence of it.

Very often, nativistic religion does not function simply to fulfill a psychological need by allowing escapism in nourishing hope for a better world to come. Religion is not necessarily escapist; it can be a mechanism of indoctrinating for action (Wilson 1973). Religion did play such a role in several nativistic movements.[6]

The notion of 'sacred' clearly contributes to social solidarity and can express itself institutionally in a religio-political organisation. Furthermore, under certain circumstances, the same socio-cultural process can function as the basis for a competing political movement (this is one form of nativism, the other being escapist). The Haitian example is of the first type. Haiti is not a unique case in this sense;

there are many other examples of nativist reactions to colonialism in the New World. However, it is different from all the companion cases in the Americas for one important reason. Although the situation in Haiti was similar to those in many other places in the New World, the historical outcome in Haiti was distinctive. It is our only example of a 'successful' nativist movement in the New World, that is, one in which the nativist movement successfully replaced the colonial political system, allowing a different segment of the population to assume political power. After the independence of Haiti in 1804, the political dimension of Voodoo can better be studied from the standpoint of state-church relationships.

STATE–CHURCH RELATIONSHIPS

Throughout the history of mankind, one encounters various types of relationship between dominant and peripheral churches and the state. In summarising and contrasting the main features of these relationships, one may be able to pinpoint the singularity of the relationship between the state and the Voodoo church in Haiti.

State–church relationships fall into two extreme models and several mitigated arrangements inbetween. One extreme model is provided by the theocratic state. In ancient Israel during the time of King Salomon and David, for example, the political leader was also considered *de facto* and by divine right the religious leader of the state (De Vaux 1965: 100–2). It was not so much that every religious man was seen as a political man, but rather that every political leader was considered a religious man. The administrative and political functions of the state were carried out by religious leaders. The laws of the nation were set according to the moral standards and beliefs of one religious group. Here the line of separation between religion and politics was very thin indeed.

The other extreme model is found in some communist states (Conquest 1968). There are examples in the communist world where the state is actively against institutionalised religions, where the political leaders are anti-religious, where the established churches are formally persecuted, are not given formal recognition, are considered illegal, and where their ministers are silenced or expelled.[7] Here the relation of the state to the church is an antagonistic one marked by open state opposition to church existence and practices.

In such a setting, the church lacks its religious freedom and maintains an ambiguous status in society.

Another state–church arrangement is demonstrated by the states that recognise the existence of pluralist religious ideologies in their midst. The United States is a case in point. The separation of the state and the church is guaranteed by the constitution, and here no church has been elevated to the status of state church. Religious leaders may, as any citizen, seek political office; religious groups, similar to any political groups, may interfere in politics to influence the decisions that may affect a particular church and its flock (Adams 1970). Here all the churches have theoretically the same status before the law.

In seventeenth century France, where one finds a different kind of state–church arrangement, the Catholic king was considered to be divinely appointed (Blet 1972). Here is another form of the separation of the state and the church. The king received much support from the church and supported church teachings and expansionist practices. The king was not considered a religious leader in the theological sense of the word, but rather a political leader with religious responsibilities.

There are still other nations that, through formal arrangements such as a concordat, concede to a particular church the status of state church. In such a situation, all the other churches have a peripheral status and do not receive the same recognition and accruing state benefits as the state church (Mecham 1966: 344–5). Here the official church may be exploited by the government or a specific statesman for secular or political reasons and is a part of the state apparatus.

Furthermore, the relation between the state and the church can be symmetrical. One example that comes to mind is the situation of Vatican City, which is a state within a state (Binchy 1941). The relationship between the Vatican and the government of Italy is similar in many ways to relationships that may exist between two autonomos states. The Vatican has its administrative governmental structure, its army and its own diplomats, who represent its long- and short-term interests in Italy and elsewhere in the world.

VOODOO AND POLITICS

The selected models of state–church relationships previously cited do not represent the situation of the Voodoo church in Haiti, but help us understand some aspects of it. When one posits the relation of church and state in the case of Voodoo, one does not mean two entities legally constituted where one recognises the existence of the other as a legitimate basis for social interaction. Rather, it is a situation in which the state pretends that Voodoo cannot function freely as a legal entity and therefore has no legal right to exist – it is forbidden by law. Ever since the independence of the country, the relation of Voodoo to the state has always been ambiguous.[8]

The political history of Voodoo is that of an underground church that has been struggling for its recognition in the fields of both religion and politics. It has not been recognised as a legitimate church, so it cannot enjoy the same religious freedom accorded to the other churches in Haiti. This is part of the ambiguity of the attitudes of the state *vis-à-vis* its native church. For that matter, the Haitian Revolution was a political but not a cultural revolution. On Independence Day, the colonists' religion was made the state religion, and the slave religion or the religion of the majority was pushed underground. International acceptance of Haitian independence no doubt forced the former slaves to opt for this halfway solution, which consisted of maintaining their former masters' religion, school system and language. This ambiguity of formally recognising the Catholic church while legally forbidding the practice of Voodoo – meanwhile using the services of the Voodoo church in matters of health and politics – has been a fundamental point of contradiction in the relations between the native church and the state throughout the history of Haiti.

Three main factors have helped shape the relations between Voodoo and politics in Haiti. First, the international press, which consistently identified the country with Voodoo – meaning cannibalism, zombi and the backwardness of its supposed cannibal practises – has maintained a psychological pressure on the government to disavow itself from the church. Second, the local bourgeoisie, eager to maintain a semblance of civilisation, has always called for the banishment of the church from the republic – the existence of Voodoo has always been an embarrassment to the Western-oriented and educated elite. Third, the Catholic church, which saw in Voodoo a competitor, pressured the state to formally outlaw the Voodoo church so as to facilitate its proselytising work (Robert 1965). The relations between the state and the Voodoo church have always been influenced implicitly or explicitly by these internal and external factors.

Since the concordat, the struggle of the Catholic church against

Voodoo has always been a major factor affecting the Voodoo church's survival. In the nineteenth century, the Catholic church engaged in abusive discursive practices and created an anti-Voodoo league (Kersuzan 1896, 1898). This strategy was judged by the Catholic clergy to be enough to eradicate the Voodoo church from the republic. In the first part of the twentieth century, as Haitian intellectuals were defending the practice of Voodoo, the Catholic church in collaboration with the state tried – this time by physical force – to rid the island of Voodoo (Peters 1941; Roumain 1937).

Voodoo is used differently by various classes in Haitian society. A way of life for the masses, it helps polarise the nation into those who appropriate it so that they can control the political arena, and the traditional bourgeoisie, who see Voodoo as a threat to its legitimacy. The political history of Voodoo is marked by this dialectical tension between the believers and the outsiders or exploiters of the church.

When the Catholic church persecutes Voodoo, it does so on behalf of the elite and with the help of the government. When the state persecutes Voodoo, it does so because of pressure from the elite and always on behalf of the Catholic church. The strength of the Catholic church reinforces elite status, and the strength of the elite reinforces Catholic church status. The relations of the Catholic church and the elite *vis-à-vis* the Voodoo church are influenced by the practices of the elite, who use Voodoo for medical and political purposes, and by the Voodoo people, who get from the elite whatever they can in terms of social rewards. Here religion as an ideology can be used to decipher social status, to diagnose social reality and to understand the history of discursive practices and the network of discursive genealogies such as developed by the Catholic clergy and the elite *vis-à-vis* Voodoo. As Houtart (1977: 267) puts it, the social actors produce, reproduce and transform social relations.

The colour question also finds its ramification in Voodoo. The mulatto elite who want to eradicate Voodoo do not wish to pass for anti-black. The black elite who want to protect the church do not want to pass for cannibal (Price-Mars 1928). The history of the perceptions of the reality as seen by these two influential segments of Haitian society no doubt influence the struggle of the church for its recognition by the state.

Although Voodoo has been outlawed, it has always remained at the centre of Haitian politics while being rejected or maintaining a marginal status. It inspired a liberation movement leading to the independence of the colony; it provided an underground organisation to fight against the elite's illegal appropriation of peasant lands; it provided guerilla leaders and rebels in the nation's fight against the US occupation (1915–34); and, more recently, its church leaders were co-opted as militiamen in the administration of the dynastic Duvalier regime (Laguerre 1982a). The following chapters provide detailed analyses of key issues in the politicisation of Voodoo in Haitian society.

2 The Evolution of Colonial Voodoo

The process of Creolisation, which began with the Spanish colonisation of Haiti, affected every aspect of the slave's life, including the organisation of his religious institutions. The emerging nativist religions also bore the mark of the emerging Creole culture. In several areas of the island, because of the kind of plantation prevalent – coffee, sugar, indigo, cotton – and the African origins of the slaves, various types of Creolised slave cults emerged. Haitian historians and ethnologists, influenced by the late Dr Jean Price-Mars – a theorist of negritude – have always argued that differences that existed in Voodoo in the beginning of the eighteenth century disappeared by the time of the Haitian Revolution (Trouillot 1970; Denis and Duvalier 1944). According to these historians and ethnologists, during the regular Voodoo meetings in which maroons and slaves participated, the Voodoo cults were unified and standardised and became a cohesive political factor for revolutionary slaves and maroons (Price-Mars 1928: 114; Denis and Duvalier 1944: 21). The underlying assumption in their writings is that ritual, theological, and organisational uniformity is necessary to achieve racial solidarity and political unity. Data provided by colonial chroniclers, missionaries and travellers allows us not only to test this hypothesis, but also to reject it.[1] Indeed, these data instead show the diversity of the cults from one region to another during the whole colonial period (Moreau de Saint-Méry 1958, I: 60–70; Malenfant 1814: 217; Drouin de Bercy 1814: 178; Descourtilz 1935: 380). This observation would be a very casual one if the recognition of these pluralist structures were not crucial to understanding the organisation and the functioning of both colonial cults and the contemporary Voodoo church.

In this ecological approach to Creolised slave religious cults during the period of the French colonisation of Haiti, I have three main purposes. First, I will document that the Haitian plantation system, ecologically different from the West African milieu, served as a basis for the emergence of various forms of syncretic Voodoo cults. Second, I will show that, because of the specific ecological niching of the plantation sites – differing from one zone to another because of their geographical location, the number and origins of people involved in plantation work, and the type and size of the plantations – various forms of Creolised slave religious cults emerged and evolved by following three distinct stages, all directly related to the three different periods in the development of the political economy of the island. Third, I will demonstrate that colonial Voodoo syncretism was the result of magical and religious acculturation of the slaves – by which I mean the process of incorporating certain symbolic items, material elements, and theological ideas borrowed from Catholicism and Indian religions into the Voodoo cults. Some of these items were incorporated as parallel magical elements to strengthen the magical and religious power inherent in Voodoo.

The word 'voodoo' is used here as a generic term, covering all the Creolised slave cults of French colonial Haiti. It is used in the same manner as one may employ the term 'Christianity' to refer to the religion of the congregations of any Christian denomination. Just as all sects within the Christian world believe in Christ, so different cults of voodooism believe in *Gran-Mèt* (the Supreme Being).

FROM AFRICAN TO SLAVE RELIGIONS

The traditional religions of Africa could hardly be perpetuated *in toto* in the New World because of the vast ecological differences between the continents. These religions developed in specific niches provided by the West African environment and met particular individual and group needs. The traditional West African religions were linked to bio-geographic niches, such as the tropical forest and savannah (Bastide 1961: 37). Each native African cult reflected the political structure of the tribe and the polygamous pattern of family life. Cult organisation was influenced by the community and its political leaders. The cult calendar followed the cycle of seasons, and appropriate ceremonies marked the harvest. Living in the settlement of a tribe could give an individual the right to participate in its cult, and membership of a tribe was most commonly gained by birth or marriage.[2]

The traditional African religions, evolved in agricultural areas and shaped by the prevalent socio-economic system in each region, were strongly rooted in the household (Parrinder 1970). These were not only the religions of the living, but also of the dead (Mbiti 1970). Ancestor worship played a role of prime importance in these communities. Furthermore, the priest's function was not only to perform or preside over ceremonies, but also to be a good medicine man. The priest, with his intimate knowledge of the West African fauna and flora, was able to use them for therapeutic purposes (Field 1937).

The Haitian plantation milieu was different in many respects from that of West Africa. Slaves from the same region in Africa were often placed on separate plantations in order to avoid possible rebellion.[3] These differences were more particularly visible in terms of population composition and natural environment. However, a large number of African countries provided slaves for the New World. According to a Jesuit missionary, Pierre François-Xavier de Charlevoix, there were:

> . . . the Senegallois, of all the Blacks the best fashioned, the easiest to discipline, and the most adapted for domestic service; the Bambaras, tallest of all, but thieves; the Aradas, those who know agriculture best, but who are the proudest; the Congos, the smallest and the most apt at fishing, but who were most prone to desert their masters; the Nagos, the most human; the Mondongos, the most cruel; the Mines, the most resolute, the most capricious, and the most subject to despair of themselves. (Cited in Herskovits 1971: 16)

Although many African territories contributed to the development of the black population of Haiti, the region of the Gold Coast and more particularly that of Dahomey seems to have been the main supplier. Paraphrasing a quotation from the Reports of the Lords of the Committee of Council appointed for Consideration of all Matters Relating to Trade and Foreign Plantation (1789), John (1958: 29) wrote:

> The reason why it was the religious conceptions of Dahomey in particular that came to prevail in Haiti is apparent from a London Report of 1789 which tells us that ten to twelve thousand slaves were exported yearly from the kingdom of Dahomey. The English exported only seven to eight hundred of these, the Portuguese about three thousand and the French the remainder, in other words more than six to eight thousand a year, who were shipped to the French Antilles, above all to Saint-Domingue, as the principal French colony of Haiti was then called.

Another observation – a linguistic one – confirms that hypothesis. Even today, Voodoo possesses several words of Dahomean origin.[4]

Indeed, some of the words that characterise the function of the Voodoo hierarchy are from the Fon language:

> The word vodoun itself is Dahomean in origin. Among the Fon speaking peoples of West Africa it signified 'spirit' or deity . . . the cult priest is usually referred to as a houngan, a Fon (Dahomean) title signifying 'spirit chief'. . . . He also is known by the title bocor, which seems to be derived from bocono, the diviner or priest of the Dahomean Fa cult. (Courlander 1960: 10)

The plantation milieu, incompatible with the survival of socio-economic African institutions, was the matrix within which Creole culture emerged. The social and structural pattern created by slavery influenced – at one level or another – the slave life from one period to another. Salient factors that shaped this pattern were forced Christianisation in certain areas, the impossibility of slaves reconstructing and making viable the polygamous African pattern of family life, the rhythm of life regularised by the plantation schedule and the interests of the colonists, the participation of the slaves in the cultural life within the slave quarter, and the absence of political power or the total dependency upon the colonists (see Hall 1971). Other ecological factors, such as the differences in environment and in population composition between rural areas and urban zones, as well as between the sugar and coffee plantations, also affected the slave culture or the emerging Creole culture (Laborie 1798). In these distinct niches various Creolised slave religions emerged.

It is not possible to understand and explain fully how these religious cults evolved without a careful analysis of the plantation system that set the pattern both of spatial and social-structural relations within the population. The history of the black man in Haiti during the period of Spanish and French colonisation is the history of his resistance to economic exploitation, political subjugation and cultural assimilation. By his sustained resistance, he was successful enough in developing his own style of a politics of survival. Thus, emergent religions bore in their roots both a religious and a political dimension (Sosis 1971). These two dimensions were strongly present in Voodoo during the entire slavery period. The plantation, day-to-day, shaped cult boundaries. The legal holidays, which ordinarily coincided with the Christian feasts, served as regular calendars for the performance of Voodoo dances.

Slave religions were a symbol of racial solidarity, and no ethnic boundaries could prevent anyone from taking part. An individual's position in the priesthood's hierarchy did not depend necessarily on his lineage, but rather on his charisma, expertise and knowledge of the therapeutic use of herbs. Until the period of the Haitian Revolution, nativist religions were practised secretly under the guise of evening dances (Métraux 1958). Some households served as the centre of performance for the family cult. I propose that, in those domestic places of worship, the African ancestors were not over-shadowed by the addition of Creole ancestors. Toward the end of the eighteenth century, some slave groups in the north invoked Makandal, a former maroon and Voodoo prophet, as one of the *loas* (spirits) of their pantheon.[5]

As the plantation economy expanded, the slave population grew; the increasing proportion of blacks to whites created more tension; and the relations between the classes became more difficult (see Bellegarde 1953). This tension created an atmosphere conducive to emerging group consciousness among the slaves. Although in the beginning colonists interpreted the Voodoo dances as innocent social gatherings, when the slaves began to protest against their servile condition the colonial administration perceived these dances as a religio-political phenomenon and outlawed them (see Moreau de Saint-Méry, 1958, III). The Creolised slave religions expressed by those dances evolved through three phrases directly related to the economic growth – not the economic development – of the island and the black demographic revolution. The economy progressed from small property holdings to large sugar plantations and finally to the collapse of the sugar industry.

FORMATION OF VOODOO CULTS

The pre-sugar revolution period is mainly characterised by a subsistence economy. This period extends from the beginning of the colonisation to the end of the seventeenth century. The economy, based on small plantations, influenced the social relations between the races. On those small plantations, indigo, cocoa, cotton, coffee and sugar cane were cultivated for local consumption and trade with metropolitan France (Redsons 1970: 13). At this early stage it seemed imprudent to colonists to develop larger individual plantations because of the political climate which included the possibility of invasion by the Spanish and English. Analysing documents relating to the early French settlers, Gabriel Debien wrote:

The early concessions were small; those at Léogane in 1680 measured 150 × 600 steps and had an area of 9 carreaux each (the carreaux is an old French unit of land, with dimensions of 100 steps to a side, equivalent to about 3.15 acres). A concessionaire was supposed to develop his land in order to retain it; once he had it under cultivation he could request another concession. (Cited in Street 1960: 117)

During this entire period the black population was smaller than the white population. The native Indian population was slowly dying out. According to Spanish records, there were '60 000 Indians' on the island (Krieger 1930: 478) at the beginning of the Spanish colonisation in 1507. The first years of the Spanish colonisation were disastrous for the Indian population. As Rainey (1941: 15) points out: 'Estimates of the population of the island at the time of the discovery range from 200 000 to 300 000, but by the time of Benzoni's visit in 1541 strife with the Spanish as well as enforced labour on the plantations had reduced the natives to 4000.' The Indian genocide did not stop until their extinction as an ethnic group. A brief survey of the population of certain parishes confirms this assertion. In 1631, there were 1074 whites, 752 blacks, and 128 metizos, mulattoes and Indians in the south (Moreau de Saint-Méry 1958, III: 1164). The census of 1681, which is the first official census of the French section of the island, gave for the population of Jérémie the following numbers: 163 whites and 117 blacks, mulattoes, metizos and Indians; for Tortuga, 168 whites, 89 blacks, and 17 mulattoes and Indians; and for Léogane, 973 whites, 625 blacks, among them 34 Indians (Moreau de Saint-Méry 1958, III: 1400, II: 708, 1111).

Because the white colonist population numerically surpassed the black during this period, the colonists did not perceive slave revolts as a great danger. There were individual revolts from time to time; however, the maroon communities were not yet a threat to the colony (see Fouchard 1972). In certain maroon settlements, Indians surpassed blacks in number. In Bahoruco, for example, the first maroons to settle there were Indians, and small groups of slaves joined them (see Debbash 1961). On the whole, slavery had not yet reached its peak of cruelty, and the blacks were not yet well enough organised to challenge the system successfully – as they did later.

The medical aspect of Voodoo was also operative, for some slaves wore talismans to prevent illness. The talisman was considered to have magical powers. Father Labat (1742, I: 488) attested to this practice: 'A black slave asked me to give him a little bag that I had taken from him before baptising him. I was informed by his master that he was known as a sorcerer'.

One of the sorcerer's functions was to serve as a medicine man. His medical knowledge derived not only from African folk medical traditions but also from Indian medical practices (Laguerre 1987a: 25). His visits to his patients were probably made secretly to avoid the colonists' reaction, but his identity was known in the slave community.[6] Labat, a Dominican missionary friar who resided in the French West Indies in the first half of the eighteenth century, observed a medicine man working on a patient:

> I was informed one night that there was a slave medicine-man in the hut of a sick woman. My first reaction was to punish him and to drive him away, but being close to the door I stopped to see what he was doing. I saw the ill slave lying on a mat. A small grotesque figure, *zemi*, was on a little seat in the midst of the hut and the medicine-man was on his knees and seemed to pray seriously in front of this figure. (Labat 1742, I: 496)

Indian figures, such as the aforementioned *zémis* found on some plantations, were probably added to cult objects for their magical powers (Moreau de Saint-Méry 1958, I: 244). Certain symbols from Catholicism, such as the sign of the cross, were certainly incorporated into early Voodoo rituals. The cults were at their first stage of development and the religious and healing aspect surpassed the emergent political dimension. The idea of a possible successful revolution was still remote, but the awareness of racial solidarity and class exploitation came with time and the forces of historical circumstances.[7]

DEVELOPMENT OF VOODOO CULTS

At the end of the seventeenth century, the western portion of Hispaniola officially became a French possession. The size of the sugar cane plantations increased, and this provided large importations of slaves, who now outnumbered the white population. In its economic and demographic parameters, this period was different from the preceding one. There was a transition from a subsistence economy to an economy oriented mainly toward sugar exportation (Pierre-Charles 1967: 16). The sugar plantation favoured the concentration of a large number of slaves in the same area, caused the desertion of some of them to maroon settlements, increased their awareness of their economic exploitation and helped develop a racial solidarity among those conscious of their subordinate status in the colony.

By now, the native Indians were almost completely exterminated as an ethnic group except for the 500 Natchez Indians that the governor of Louisiana, Mr Salvert, had sold to French colonists. The majority of them were women who were employed as domestics (Moreau de Saint-Méry 1958, I: 95). On the eve of the French Revolution, the population of the island presented the following spectrum: 30 836 whites, 27 548 free coloured and 465 429 slaves.[8]

It was during the sugar revolution period that the Creolised religious cults started to be more systematically organised as a group activity, and a large number of plantations took their permanent form in terms of crops raised. At this point, it is useful to identify the variables that played a part in developing these Creole cults, even if they did not all influence the cults with the same intensity. These variables can be summarised thus:

1. The type, location, and size of the plantation. I earlier pointed out that the coffee plantation niche (mountains) was different from the sugar plantation niche (plains). The difference is marked in terms of geographical situation, size of the slave population and work schedule.
2. The composition of the slave population – the number of Africans in relation to that of Creoles – is significant because it was related to the ethnic origin of the larger group of slaves in the area or in the plantation.
3. The presence or absence of former African priests. These priests were known as such in Africa and continued to hold some of their privileges on the plantations. They provided cultural continuity as far as the evolution of the Creole cults was concerned.
4. The presence or absence of trained leaders from other islands. For example, there is some evidence that Boukman and Plymouth, two maroon leaders, probably came from Jamaica, and Santyague and Don Pedro, two Voodoo priests, from Santo Domingo. Another maroon leader and Voodoo priest, Padréjean – who was influential in the region of Port-de-Paix – came either from Cuba or Santo Domingo (Moreau de Saint-Méry 1958).
5. Proximity or remoteness and size of maroon communities. In certain regions of the colony, maroons participated often in

evening Voodoo dances organised by plantation slaves. Also, in Bahoruco, the maroons shared the settlement with Indians, which explains the presence of some Indian artifacts in the Voodoo cults practised in this region.

6. The slaves of the religious orders. These slaves were more exposed than other slaves to Catholic rituals. Religious orders such as the Carmelites, Dominicans, Franciscans, Brothers of Charity and Jesuits started to settle in Haiti by the end of the seventeenth century and the beginning of the eighteenth century.[9] In Cap-Français before the first expulsion of the Jesuits in 1763, a Jesuit missionary, Father Boutin, known as the pastor of the slaves, started to organise them and instruct them in catechism.[10] The first *Pères savannes* (bush priests) who travelled the country around 1797 probably came from this group.

The diversity of slave cults was clearly revealed for the first time by an anonymous author around 1750:

> They became excessively exalted when they meditate a wicked plan. The chief of the plot becomes so ecstatic that he loses consciousness; when he regains consciousness, he claims that his god has spoken to him and has commended the enterprise, but as they do not worship the same god, they hate each other and spy on each other reciprocally, and these plans are almost always denounced. (Cited in Simpson 1970: 234)

The diversity of Voodoo cults was related to the slaves' past religious experiences. Father Charlevoix (1730, I: 366) gave some details about the African religious background of the slaves: 'The Congos were converted to Christianity by the Portuguese 200 years ago; their kings have always been Christians since this time, and many of those Blacks are baptised. Some Senegalese close to Morocco are Muslims and circumcised. The Aradas are in the darkest darkness of idolatry and worship the snake.'

The presence of Muslims among the slave population was also reported by Colonel Malenfant (1814: 215): 'Some colonists assured me that they possessed Muslim slaves.'

Toward the middle of the eighteenth century, a large number of slaves from Whydah were brought to the island. This region is known for the role played by the snake in the cult:

> In 1727 the King of Dahomey 'smashed' the little kingdom of Whydah and turned its capital into a huge slave emporium which

was frequented by slavers right up to the second half of the last century. It has been reckoned that 10 000 slaves were sold annually at Whydah. To cross the few miles of dune and marsh which divides this town from the coast, is to fall prey to a vision of those long caravans of men, women and children, who here took their last steps on the continent of their birth. (Métraux 1972: 26)

The arrival of the slaves from Whydah brought another element to the Creole cults practised in certain regions of the colony. The snake was present where Whydah slaves formed the majority or where one of them officiated as a priest.

Moreau de Saint-Méry describes two types of Voodoo practised by the slaves.[11] He evidently speaks about the cults that were primarily known in the regions of Port-au-Prince and Cap-Français, where he lived while in the colony. According to Moreau de Saint-Méry (1958, I: 64), Voodoo 'means the existence of an all powerful and supernatural being on whom depends whatever goes on in the world.' Two ministers – representative of the spirits and known as queen and king – were part of the hierarchy of the cult. The faithful manifested blind obedience to them. Before the ceremony took place, 'with hands placed in those of the king and queen, they renew the promise of secrecy which is the foundation of the association, and it is accompanied by every thing horrible that delirium has been able to devise to make it more impressive' (Moreau de Saint-Méry 1958, I: 64). During the ceremony, a box containing a snake was exposed to everyone's view. The ceremony consisted of the offering of food, evocations in which each asked the god to fulfil his needs, and sacred dances that led some to be possessed by their spirit protectors.

The second cult that Moreau de Saint-Méry describes was somewhat different from the first one as exemplified by the Don Pedro Dance:

Who will believe that Voodoo gives place to something further which also goes by the name of dance? In 1768, a slave of Petit-Goave, of Spanish origin, abusing the credulity of the blacks, by superstitious practices gave them an idea of a dance, analogous to that of the Voodoo, but where the movements are more hurried. To make it even more effective the slaves place in the rum, which they drink while dancing, well crushed gun-powder. One has seen this dance, called Dance to Don Pedro, or simply Don Pedro, induce death in the slaves; and the spectators themselves, electrified by the spectacle of this convulsive exercise, share the drunkenness of the actors, and hasten by their chant and a quickened measure, a crisis which is in some way common to them. It has been necessary to forbid them from dancing Don Pedro under grave penalty, but sometimes ineffectually. (Moreau de Saint-Méry 1958, I: 68)

The description by Colonel Malenfant (1814: 216) also has its singularity: 'There exists among the Voodoo practitioners a big snake, placed in a big wooden box, that one shows during the ceremonies. The faithful takes an oath of secrecy to the priestess and dances until one experiences spirit possession'.

The description of Voodoo that we have from the colonial period allows us to identify the main variables upon which the cults were organised (Malenfant 1814: 217; Drouin de Bercy 1814: 178; Descourtilz 1935: 380). The Creolised slave cults shared a certain number of common features and were distinguished from one region to another by some uncommon specific features. The following six main features might be found in any slave cult in colonial Haiti:

1. The belief in monotheism, that is, in a supreme being.
2. Spirit possession as the climax of every ceremony.
3. The centre post, sometimes a tree, through which occurs the mystical communication with the spirits.
4. The religion is a danced ceremony.
5. The *vèvè* (drawing), symbol of *loas* (spirits).
6. The offering of food to the *loas* (*manger-loas*).

Some features, found in certain regions, were absent in others:

1. The development of the ceremony: The ritual procedure was not identical everywhere. This was partly due to the diversity of local traditions.
2. The functions of the priest: the presence of a priest and/or a priestess. The priest was a spiritual and political leader and/or a medicine man.
3. The symbolic number of the drums and other musical instruments.
4. The composition of the Voodoo pantheon and the attributes of the *loas*: in certain regions, certain *loas* were venerated; in others, they were unknown. The colour preferred by the spirits and the type of food offering also differed from one place to another.
5. The incorporation of Indian artifacts and of ritual objects or symbols of the Catholic church.
6. The presence or absence of the snake or of a symbol of the snake. The snake did exist in the decorum of the cult in some regions. Where it did exist, the snake had a symbolic meaning, like the

dove and the fish in Christian liturgy. It was less the creature that was important than the symbol it represented. It is as incorrect to say, as colonial writers thought, that slaves worshipped snakes as to affirm that Christians worship fishes and doves.

These variables influenced in one way or another the formation of the various colonial Voodoo cults. No doubt by the time of the Haitian Revolution, these cults had fuelled the political consciousness building and the rebellious spirit of the slaves. Colonists, as soon as they perceived the political role played by slave dances, outlawed them and prosecuted both those who allowed them and those who participated in them.[12] Voodoo cults became the first organised foci of open resistance to slavery. As Drouin de Bercy observes: 'Don Pedro, like Voodoo, is a very dangerous secret society. The goal of its members is to kill or expel all the whites from the colony. Members never reveal the secrets of the group to non-initiates' (cited in Paul 1962: 236).

Colonial Voodoo was basically a plantation-based institution, except in the case of the maroons. There existed no Voodoo pope to regularise the colonial cult, to decide the orthodoxy of the doctrine or to standardise the ritual. While France was busying herself with war at home, the Voodoo groups became cells of political organisation for revolutionary blacks and mulattoes.

EXPLOSION OF VOODOO CELLS

The ceremony of Bois-Caiman, which occurred on 14 August 1791, marked the decline of the one prosperous economy of the colony. The contradictions inherent in the slavery system were pushed to their extreme and provided the social climate necessary for a revolution. Fires started in the northern plantations by slaves forced a great number of colonists to leave the colony in search of refuge in the US, Jamaica and Cuba.[13] The rise of the black population to its peak – outnumbering by far the small group of colonists – was parallel to the decline in the economy. The gross national product in 1789 evaluated at 175 990 000 pounds fell in 1801 to 65 352 039 pounds (Justin 1826: 500).

In 1793, the colonial administration proclaimed the general emancipation of the slaves. As a result, the social atmosphere and the work schedule in the plantations underwent significant changes. Maroons freely mingled with the freedmen, and the Voodoo cults, practised more openly, continued to be a focus of resistance against the colonists. Also during this period, the first bush priests appeared. They were probably former slaves who had belonged to the plantations of religious orders and thus knew about Catholicism and other Christian rituals.[14] Toussaint Louverture himself learned Latin while he was working at the Hospital of the Brothers of Charity in Cap-Français. Father Constantin de Luxembourg, former Apostolic prefect, in a letter to Reverend Grégoire (9 April 1799), affirms to have known 'Toussaint, slave at the Hospital of the Brothers of Charity, where he used to be a waiter when I came there to get dinner' (Cabon 1933: 44). The function of the bush priests was to recite psalms and Catholic Latin prayers, recognised for their magical powers.

The first Voodoo temples appeared during this period. In the maroon settlements, Voodoo sanctuaries appeared earlier. As soon as households were formed, spirit protectors of these households were venerated by its members. The various Voodoo traditions that developed in the colony were not standardised. Reciprocal acculturation and syncretism occurred; yet each Voodoo cult had its own traditions (Sosis 1971).

Political circumstances caused neighbouring Voodoo priests to gather around an influential political leader of the same region. This compromise, however, did not cause ritual unity and uniformity in Voodoo. There was unity on the goal to be reached – liberation from metropolitan France. For greater efficacy, the unity of political action was perceived as essential. Voodoo priests of various religious traditions accompanied leaders such as Biassou, Halaou and Romaine-La-Prophétesse on the battlefield (Mennesson-Rigaud 1958: 63–64; Justin 1826: 62). There was some competition between priests around the same leader, political prestige being regarded as vital for attracting followers.

RELIGIOUS ACCULTURATION OF THE SLAVES

The slaves' religious traditions were the product of a slow and long process of Creolisation. Slaves were not acculturated to the European cultures as such, but to the emergent Creole culture (Laguerre 1970). The colonists themselves were also affected by this process of Creolisation.

Despite the general policy of the colony to separate slaves coming from the same region, neighbouring African priests in some areas kept them together by organising the cult around known spirits of their country. Other spirits were incorporated as a reflection of the congregation's religious needs. To understand the formation of slave cults, it is more important to know the prestige of the priest and his birthplace than the number of slaves of the same origin.

Mennesson-Rigaud considered Voodoo centres a good index to identifying cultural foci in Haiti. Her observation is perhaps perceptive in some respects and needs to be tested on other grounds:

> Blacks being little by little rooted in Haiti where they were brought created foci of belief which reflected their African origin that until the present day can be found because of Voodoo. Thus one finds Anmines in Artibonite and Ester, Ibos in the South West (around Anse à Veau, L'Asile . . .), Kita around Cayes, Congos in La Vallée region, Jacmel, Gonaives and Léogane; Mandingues in the Plain of the North, and finally Aradas predominate in the north eastern part of Port-au-Prince, Cul-de-Sac. (Mennesson-Rigaud 1958: 53)

In the regions mentioned, there evidently was divergence in religious patterns. Because of the dearth and paucity of materials published on Voodoo practices outside of Port-au-Prince, it is still too early to be able to demonstrate adequately the ritual and theological contours of the Voodoo cults in colonial Haiti.

The proximity of the Catholic church and Indian religions meant that the slaves had experienced some form of religious acculturation (Herskovits 1971; Bastide 1970). For example, the presence of the chromolithographs of Catholic saints in a Voodoo centre was a singular mark of this acculturation. However, only those Catholic saints who were known to them were incorporated in the repertoire of their supernatural beings.

To understand the symbolism of the Creole religions, one needs more than a description of the cult centres in terms of objects present there. It is as important to analyse the *weltanschauung* of the worshippers as to study their behaviour under extreme duress, such as death or illness. When a slave died, secret Voodoo prayers were offered to protector *loas*, but they might also ask a Catholic priest to say a mass for the dead. Here the Catholic mass was understood as a magical ritual, and chickens were symbolically presented to the priest. For the slaves, such a mass was believed to be a *manger-loa* (food for the spirits). Father Labat (1742, IV: 162) described this feature well, even if he did not understand its meaning, when he wrote: 'All the friends and compatriots of the dead do not miss, as soon as they can, to go and pray to God on his tomb, and if they have some money or chickens, they give it to the priest to say a mass for the dead.'

The historical records that we have do not reveal the behaviour of slaves in various extreme situations. However, as an example, I have chosen the Haitian Revolution, during which blacks burned a number of Catholic churches. This example seems to indicate that slaves did not consider Catholicism superior to the Voodoo cult and that there was no danger in its being so thought. Cabon (1933: 91), quoting Father Lecun, a missionary who lived in Haiti during the troubles, wrote, 'All the churches, except those of Port-au-Prince, Saint-Marc and Cayes, have been burned a long time ago; the last three certainly will be burned.'

Catholicism was perceived by some as the 'magic of the whites' (Laguerre 1969: 133). During the revolutionary wars for the liberation of the country, slaves had more confidence in the god of their ancestors, who protected their interests, than in the Catholic saints, who represented the interests of the colonists.

I have already mentioned the fact that Indian artifacts such as *zémis* were certainly used in some maroon settlements, particularly in Bahoruco, where both Indians and blacks lived together for a long time. Those elements were incorporated mostly for their magical power. Up to the present day, in the region of Jacmel, one finds Indian artifacts in the Voodoo temples as part of their sacred and religious paraphernalia.

The colonial *vèvès* were also an adaptation to the ecology of the island. For more magical efficacy, Christian crosses were added to them. In a letter to a Haitian ethnologist the well-known specialist on West African religions, Geoffrey Parrinder, wrote, 'The word *vèvè* comes from the sister languages Fon of Abomey and Porto Norvo. *Vèvè* means: *farine de maïs assaisonée d'huile de palme* (flour of corn mixed with palm-oil). *Vèvè* are often found on altars and symbols representing spirits' (cited in Paul 1962: 300).

Some slaves accepted Catholicism only as a magical ritual, auxiliary to their ancestors' cults, rather than as a way of life. They perceived of Catholicism as a parallel or alternative religion. A recognition of Catholicism as a superior religion would have meant an acceptance of the status quo insofar as it was perceived as representing exclusively the interests of the colonists. The response of the slaves throughout the colonial period was rather one of resistance. If certain traits of

Christianity were selected and incorporated in Voodoo, this process was due to *eco-socialisation*, that is, a continual adaptation to a milieu in continual process of Creolisation.

The acculturation of whites to Creole food was simply a biological adaptation; the presence of the picture of a saint, a rosary or a *zémi* in a Voodoo sanctuary could have had a magical, religious and political meaning. Thus, resistance to slavery and the politics of survival are meaningful to understanding the process of religious acculturation of the slaves.

Colonial Voodoo syncretism was more a magical than a profoundly religious one. By this I mean that more than anything else, there was a simple accumulation of gestures (the sign of the cross), formulae (psalms, Catholic prayers), images of saints and other cultic objects. This magical syncretism was a kind of precaution: it was thought to be better to rely upon two magics instead of one.

SUMMARY

From this discussion of the formation and the development of Voodoo cults in French colonial Haiti, we can isolate three ideas. First, no traditional African religions survived because of the differences between the social organisation in the West African environment and the slavery system in the New World plantation milieu.

Second, in the Haitian plantation milieu, various Voodoo cults emerged, related to specific niches. These cults shared some common features, but also had some differences that allow us to classify them as distinct. The development of these various cults passed through three phases, singularly related to the economic growth and the demographic evolution of the colony. During the first stage, the accent was more on the role of the priest as a medicine man; periodic Voodoo meetings occurred and contributed to the politics of survival of the slaves. In the second phase, Voodoo carried out both a political and a religious function, favoured the political group consciousness of slaves, and enforced and strengthened their racial solidarity. In the third phase, Voodoo became the focus of political and underground activities and served as the channel to carry out the leaders' political ideology which was the total and unconditional liberation of Haiti from France.

Against the Haitian ethnologists such as disciples of Price-Mars who argue that at the beginning of the colonisation there was diversity in the cult but by the time of the Haitian Revolution the cult was standardised by political circumstances, I propose that doctrinal unity and ritual uniformity in Voodoo never existed. There was, however, unity among the slaves based on race–class solidarity for an effective political action. The blacks of the south (bastion of the mulattoes) clearly had very little contact with those of the north. Even when slaves gathered around a regional leader, they were not motivated by the desire for ritual uniformity but for the sharing of political goals. Thus, Voodoo has to be considered as a generic term, covering these various Creolised cults.

Third, contact with Indian and Christian religions had not necessarily caused a formal religious acculturation. In several instances there was, rather, a magical syncretism–accumulation of relics because of their magical potency. This syncretism was related to the environment in which it occurred (proximity to Indians, Catholic saints venerated in nearby places). The rationale of this strategy is that in magic, it is better to be safe than sorry.

3 Marronage and Voodoo

During the period of the French colonisation of Haiti, the two groups of people who did not live on the plantations were the absentee landlords and the maroons. The landlords lived in France and had managers who took care of their holdings in the colony. Maroons were runaway slaves who either established autonomous settlements or were able to 'lose' themselves in various ways among the free people in the colony; some of the former returned from time to time to raid neighbouring plantations.

Marronage existed in numerous places in the New World and in various forms, depending on the physical environment, the size of the white and black populations, the type of production prevalent and other historical circumstances. In Haiti, the mountains situated on the frontier between the French and the Spanish parts of the island were some of the privileged places where maroons settled their camps (Fouchard 1972: 424).

The student who intends to analyse the social organisation of maroon groups and communities in colonial Haiti faces a series of problems due mainly to a lack of primary and reliable documentation of various aspects of their social life. Strategically speaking, maroon groups functioned as 'secret societies', that is, only maroons knew the details of their organisation. Unfortunately, we have very few testimonies from the maroons themselves.[1] The records we have are from testimonies of soldiers who participated in raids against specific maroon communities and from colonial newspapers (see Fouchard 1972). These documents are more or less limited to observations about the physical environment of settlements, approximate number of maroons in a camp, places of origin, names, ages, their political and military tactics and their means of subsistence (Moreau de Saint-Méry 1958). We must use such accounts with critical eyes because they may be tainted by prejudice and ethnocentrism. In their panic, the colonial administration was more preoccupied with eradicating the maroons from the colony and solving the troubles that they caused on the plantations or on the public roads than with understanding how maroon communities were structurally organised.

Marronage was a central fact in the life of the colony, not only because of maroon military power and the number of slaves who constantly joined them, but also because of the danger inherent in

39

expeditions to destroy revolutionary centres of these fugitive slaves. Any study centred upon the slaves must also consider this phenomenon of marronage; for wherever there were slaves, there were also maroons (Schoelcher 1842: 119). Living in free camps or on the fringes of port cities, they were a model for the slaves to imitate, embodying the desires of most of the slaves. What the slaves used to say in *sotto voce* on the plantations, they were able to say aloud in the maroon settlements.

Various types of marronage existed in the colony, from simple vagrancy on public roads and marronage in cities to well-organised bush maroon settlements (Debien 1966: Debbash 1961). Our task will be to differentiate between them in order to show the role played by each in the boycott of the slave plantation system and in the struggle for the independence of the colony. In this chapter, I first locate geographically the settlements of some maroon communities in Haiti; second, determine their size and how they functioned; and third, discuss the influence of marronage on the formation of colonial Voodoo.

RURAL MARRONAGE

One way for a slave to manifest his disagreement and to protest against the slave system was to leave the plantation and begin a maroon's life. The immediate causes for such a departure were many. Slaves ran away when they were in trouble with their masters, when they did not receive enough food for their subsistence, when they were forced to work day and night, when other maroons forced them to escape, or when they felt the need to fight against the slave system (Fouchard 1972: 33–56). But where does the term 'maroon' originate? According to Father Margat, (1827: 347), a Jesuit missionary who worked in colonial Haiti around 1750:

> It comes from the Spanish word 'Simarron' (cimarron) which means monkey. One knows that those animals live in the woods and go out only secretly to eat fruits that are in the neighbouring places of their retreat. . . . It is the name that Spaniards gave to their fugitive slaves, and this name is also adopted in the French colonies.

Marronage began quite early in colonial Haiti. We know that well before the French colonisation of the island, newly arrived slaves took refuge in the eastern part of the island. They later came out periodically to initiate disturbances on the surrounding plantations. According to Father Charlevoix (1730, II: 38), another Jesuit missionary, 'in 1665, at seven leagues from the capital, lived nearly 1200 men in a maroon settlement. Their inaccessible retreat located on a mountain (Bahoruco) attracted slaves of the city and around.' From the first years of slavery on the island, Indians and slaves had run away to inaccessible mountains, and throughout the colonial period, every mountain in Haiti was used at one time or another by fugitive slaves (see Moreau de Saint-Méry 1958). The following are sites, according to Moreau de Saint-Méry and other chroniclers where maroon settlements were located:

1. *Parish of Vallières*. This parish contained the Mulatto Bluff at the bottom of which flowed the Mulatto River. Vallières, a village close to the frontier of Santo Domingo, was the main town of the parish. In fact, the Mulatto River provided a line of separation for the two colonies. The name Mulatto River was given by M Saffray de Tournemine, provost-marshal, who while pursuing some fugitive slaves lost a mulatto, who was killed on the banks of this river (Moreau de Saint-Méry 1958, I: 157).

   Vallières was not a large parish; but like the other parishes of the north, it was a prosperous one. The main exporting crop grown there was coffee. Vallières produced about one and a half million pounds of coffee per year during the second half of the eighteenth century. There were about 100 plantations and a population of 160 whites, 160 freed men, and approximately 2000 slaves (Moreau de Saint-Méry 1958, I: 161).

   Some bluffs and hillocks found in this parish had names that remind one of the experience of maroons who lived there. For example, there was a Peak of Blacks, Peak of Candlesticks, Peak of Darkness and Crest of Congos. Polydor, one of the maroon chiefs in this parish, was active for almost ten years – colonists were successful in killing him and dispersing his band around 1734. It was a temporary dispersion, for shortly after his death, the maroons reorganised and continued their attacks on nearby plantations (Moreau de Saint-Méry 1958, I: 163).

2. *Parish of Saint-Louis du Nord*. The high mountain of Tarare was the privileged place of settlement of the maroons of this parish. Around 1679, about 25 maroons were living on this mountain. Their principal leader was Padréjean, a former Spanish slave who had killed his master. There were also other camps in the nearby

parishes of Port-Margot and Petit Saint-Louis (Moreau de Saint-Méry 1958, I: 666). The main place of retreat for these maroons was on Tortuga Island. In case of an attack by the colonial administration they fled back there by boat.

3. *Parish of Trou.* On the eve of the French Revolution, this parish possessed 33 sugar refineries that produced about five million pounds of refined sugar per year (Moreau de Saint-Méry 1958, I: 182). There was also a brick factory, four sugar mills, 150 coffee refineries and a great number of gardens to feed the inhabitants. This parish contained many places difficult of access to white colonists. Sheer mountains, cliffs and dark corners close to Santo Domingo became maroon settlements. They established themselves and lived there for a long time.

In 1777, in the district of Ecrevisses, the maroon chief Canga attacked neighbouring plantations with his band. Another maroon chief, Gillot – known as Yaya – who had been settled for a long time with his band on a mountain of the Parish of Trou, was captured in September 1787 during an unsuccessful attack on a plantation (Moreau de Saint-Méry 1958, I: 183).

4. *Parish of Limonade.* A well-organised maroon camp was established on Morne à Mantègre, one of the mountains of the parish of Limonade. The colonists, who sought to attack them for five years, could not secure any co-operation from the *affranchis* (freedmen) who saw the maroons as their possible allies. However, during the month of June 1724, the chief maroon, Colas Jambes Coupées, was captured, and his band dispersed. He was kidnapped on the Morne à Mantègre close to the village of Tannerie between Grande Rivière and Limonade, and executed in Bois-de-Lance (Moreau de Saint-Méry 1958, I: 207).

5. *The District of Bahoruco.* From the beginning of the colony, Bahoruco had been the place where Indian and black maroons settled. They were expelled several times by colonists and the colonial army, but they never failed to come back. Maroons had lived there during the colonial era for more than 85 years, remarks Moreau de Saint-Méry (1958, III: 1131). In 1691 maroons who were quartered in Bahoruco invaded and pillaged the plain of Cul-de-Sac. Their aim was to kill all the colonists of these plantations. During March, 1702, M de Galliffet sent 15 men to expel the maroons from Bahoruco. This military expedition killed three maroons and captured 11; the others fled to Santo Domingo. The commanding officer of Cul-de-Sac, M Dubois, destroyed the

camp once again in 1717 and forced the rebels to flee to Santo Domingo. In 1719, they were again settled in Bahoruco, and during a skirmish, the chief of the band – Michel – was captured. The major of the Jacmel militia, M Charles Beaudoin, accompanied by some inhabitants, fought the maroons and succeeded in capturing 46 of them. In 1733, 32 others were captured at the same place (Moreau de Saint-Méry 1958, III: 1131).

The mountain of Bahoruco was very appropriate for marronage because of its proximity to Santo Domingo – and because the bluffs made access to the mountain difficult. Throughout the colonial period, this mountain attracted a great number of plantation slaves and was considered a threat to the survival of the colony by the colonial authorities. Bahoruco was the oldest, the most populous and the best organised of the maroon settlements in colonial Haiti.

6. *The District of Grand-Bois*. The district of Grand-Bois, which is formed of a series of bluffs, was situated in the parish of Mirebalais. Surrounding hillocks and rivers made it difficult of access. In addition, it had the advantage of being close to the frontier of Santo Domingo where the maroons could escape in case of danger. From time to time, the maroons pillaged plantations of Cul-de-Sac and the plain of Mirebalais in routine raids. They attracted slaves from neighbouring plantations to the camp. In 1740, they were attacked by the provost-marshal of Cul-de-Sac, M Marillet, commanding 22 army men. Seven maroons were killed, 14 captured, and 23 fled to Santo Domingo (Moreau de Saint-Méry 1958, III: 1131).

7. *Parish of Nippes*. The parish of Nippes was surrounded by mountains, which were covered with small forests and were used as maroon camps, thereby attracting neighbouring plantation slaves (Archives des Colonies C⁹ B 16, 1764).

8. *Parish of Grande Anse*. The mountains of the parish of Grande Anse were also used by maroons. In 1720, the governor ordered them expelled (Moreau de Saint-Méry 1958, III: 1395). Despite attacks by the colonists, several camps remained in various places in the mountains. When the maroons were attacked and felt that they were in danger, they fled to Mt Macaya, the highest mountain in the south.

9. *The District of Plymouth*. A maroon chief, Plymouth, gave his name to this district, and the district was for a long time a stronghold of the maroons. Plymouth, a black slave from Jamaica,

had been purchased and brought to the island by an inhabitant of Cayes. Running away from his master's plantation, he became the chief of a maroon band. Ever since the colonial period the district has been identified with his name because of his notorious reputation as a troublemaker (see Fouchard 1972: 484).

URBAN MARRONAGE

The maroons did not all live in the mountains. Some, after a brief stay there, returned to the plantation areas or to the cities. The social atmosphere and anonymity of cities provided a secure niche for urban maroons (see Fouchard 1972). Indeed, several maroons established themselves in the cities, losing themselves in the crowd of the enfranchised. As is pointed out in this memoir:

> One often finds blacks that one may have good reason to believe that they are slaves. But although every colonist has the right to obtain information as to whether these blacks are free and how they were freed, the colonist prefers to believe what the blacks say about their status. For nobody wants to pay the price for a trial to contest the state of a man who could be actually a freedman. As soon as a black live(s) for two or three years in a district, claiming that he is a freedman, he is usually recognised as such by everyone. (Mémoire de la Chambre d'Agriculture du Port-au-Prince, 1764, p. 1)

In cities, maroons practised minor professions – for example, some were musicians and worked in taverns owned by the enfranchised. Others were carpenters, masons and the like.[2]

Cities such as Cap-Français, Saint-Marc, Port-au-Prince, Jacmel, Léogane and Cayes, because of their size, afforded maroons the opportunity to live anonymously. In Port-au-Prince, they lived mainly at Mt Hospital (Gazette de Saint-Domingue, 1764) and at Belair (Laguerre 1976a). The city of Ouanaminthe also provided a haven for fugitive slaves (Supplique des Habitants du Fort-Dauphin 1758). In these cities, maroons were able to organise their dances and to meet new friends and comrades. In Cap-Français, for example, 'blacks organised their dances' in the La Fossette neighbourhood (Moreau de Saint-Méry 1958, I: 543). Marronage in the cities was not only a form of resistance to economic exploitation, but was also the expression of the struggles of the blacks to maintain and develop their folk culture.

NOMADIC MARRONAGE

The third category of maroons was that of the vagrants, and two types of maroon can be distinguished in this group. First, there existed those who left for a while and returned later to the plantations to which they belonged. This practice seems to have been quite common among slaves and colonists did not usually consider such departures dangerous for the plantation economy. It was routine practice that when a fugitive slave wanted to return to his master's plantation, he would ask a priest or another respected person to accompany him in order to avoid being beaten by his master (Fouchard 1972: 384). Colonists interpreted such an escape for one or two days or even a week or a month as an 'act of laziness and libertinage' (V . . . de C . . . 1803, I: 240). Debien (1966: 7) names such a marronage the *petit marronage* to distinguish it from the *grand marronage*.

Second, there existed maroons who left the plantations forever and who were not settled definitely either in a city or in a bush maroon settlement. They were to be found everywhere on the public roads, in rural areas or in the cities, although not attached to a particular place. They were revolutionaries who stole (mainly from colonists' plantations or houses) what they needed for their subsistence. In a sense, their resistance to slavery was total. They did not want to do anything that might contribute to the maintenance of slavery. As reported in this memoir, their existence was known to the colonial administration.

One of the reasons which facilitates and multiplies in Haiti the escape of the slaves is the impossibility to distinguish in markets, in the streets, and on the roads, the slave who escapes or who walks without permission from one with permission of his master. For it is very easy to counterfeit the formula in the bond that one gives to the slave and which constitutes his permit. In the colony it is very easy also for the slave to get a permit from his comrades who know how to write. With this kind of passport, blacks come openly into the cities to sell their products and to buy provisions. (Mémoire sur les Marrons, 1778).

SIZE AND ESTABLISHMENT OF MAROON COMMUNITIES

Maroon settlements were not all the same size. The size of a camp depended on its geographical location and its age. Settlements established in the mountains close to Santo Domingo had, in general, a larger population than the others because the maroons could flee to Santo Domingo in case of an enemy attack. A settlement would become known to the colonists only when the maroons began their attacks on nearby plantations, and in general, it took maroon settlements from one to five years to become known to the colonists. Maroons generally started to raid the neighbouring plantations when their camps had between 10 and 50 members (Moreau de Saint-Méry 1958).

No maroon settlement was exactly the regrouping of a particular African tribe – however in some settlements, one ethnic group predominated at some point in camp history. A maroon camp incorporated newly arrived Africans as well as Creole slaves (Debbash 1961). Even if Creole was used in their common meetings to allow mutual understanding, individuals used their native language among themselves.

The escape of the newly arrived Africans and non-Creole or Creole plantation slaves to maroon camps was not accomplished in the same manner (Manigat 1977). The first slaves ran away during the seasoning period – before they were sold to their respective masters – and joined the first band that welcomed them. Slaves who had worked for a while on the plantations had more calculated departures – they knew where they wanted to go, and they knew more or less the identity of the members of a particular band and what types of tools and other things they had to take with them, for such information was exchanged during the Saturday Voodoo dances in which maroons and plantation slaves participated. Psychologically, it was harder for the plantation slaves to run away because of their friendships with other slaves and because of their wives and children – and sometimes because of their own property (gardens, huts, cattle). When they made the decision to leave, their departure was often well calculated. On this subject, Dutertre (1667: 536) wrote:

They never run away without having put some order in their private affairs. That is why they bring with them tools like bill-hooks, axes and knives; they bring also clothes, a good amount of big millet, and go to the highest places in the mountains where they clear woods and make gardens by planting manioc and yams. Before being able to have their own subsistence, every night they come down close to the plantations and plantation slaves bring to them what they need to eat. When they cannot have the help of some other slaves, they come proudly at night to steal on the plantations and take everything that comes under their hands; some steal even the guns and swords that belong to colonists.

Most of the plantations experienced a continual exodus of slaves to the maroon camps and frequently suffered damage from maroon raids (Debien 1966).

MAROON POLITICAL SYSTEMS

In colonial Martinique as well as in Haiti, each maroon band was organised around a chief, known as a general or governor (Arch. Col. en général XIII, F 90). Ordinarily, the chief was an individual from the ethnic group whose members were in the majority. This was not a strict rule, however: other factors also influenced the selection of a chief. First, the band had to reassure itself that the newly elected was not a spy sent by colonists. Leaders were often elected because of their kingly descent; others were chosen because they were Voodoo priests; still others had been overseers on the plantations or had displayed qualities of leadership there; some were chosen because they were charismatic leaders who were fluent in Creole, French or Spanish. In certain regions, the entire band took part in the nomination of a chief, but more often, the chief emerged as a strongman without being elected, by imposing his personality on the group. When a regional chief was elected, all the neighbouring bands took part.[3]

Political circumstances did not allow all the maroon bands to have one common headquarters where they could meet to make corporate decisions and from where they could disseminate information to dissident factions. Each maroon camp developed its own policies and tactics concerning the organisation of its group and its relations with the surrounding plantations and the colonial administration. However, even if maroons formed separate bands, a powerful chief sometimes grouped around himself all the bands in the neighbouring region. Such was the case of Plymouth in the south (Fouchard 1972).

The leader's political role included fostering group unity, being sufficiently informed to alert the band to danger and leading flights to Santo Domingo or to Tortuga Island. The leader resolved disagreements between maroons and distributed the portions of land given to all to cultivate to meet subsistence needs. He also supported the worship of Voodoo *loa* (spirits).

The maroon chief was a military man, experienced in guerilla warfare. He placed his men in remote stations to guard the maroon settlement and met periodically with the chiefs of neighbouring bands and clandestinely with plantation slaves and overseers. With the intelligence gathered from them, he determined what plantations to pillage and when to attack them.[4]

Two documents dating from the colonial period describe the security measures maroons took to protect their camps:

> To become a Maroon he goes to join other slaves, who subsist in bands in the woods, fortified in kinds of retrenched camps, closed by palissades wickered with lianas and surrounded with ditches twelve to fifteen feet deep, eight to ten wide, and protected by sharpened posts (Archives du Ministère des Colonies, Correspondance Générale, Saint-Domingue C⁹ 2è série Carton XXXIII).
>
> Maroons had as remote stations huts where two men could fall back to another hut and successively fall back until they reached the corpus of the troop. Their sentinels were dogs which they had in great number, and Spaniards bought weapons and munitions for maroons in the French part of the island. (Moreau de Saint-Méry 1958, III: 1131)

The typical maroon settlement was organised to fit the specific needs of guerilla warfare: they had to organise their camps in expectation of an enemy attack and in order to protect their gardens, maroons preferred to confront their enemies – exile in Santo Domingo was contemplated only as a final option in case of real danger.

In the cities, maroons had an informal underground government. The band was not attached to a specific place, as in the case of mountain maroons. They constituted gangs, which functioned clandestinely. Some lived in anonymity with the complicity of the enfranchised. The public meetings in which they participated were the Voodoo dances and the markets. The urban maroon groups did not come out of hiding until after the slaves of the north began the revolutionary war. In Léogane around 1797, for example, Romaine-La-Prophétesse emerged from anonymity with his band (Justin 1826: 62).

ECONOMIC ORGANISATION

For their subsistence, maroons depended heavily but not exclusively on their own plots of land and on what they could steal from the plantations (Moreau de Saint-Méry 1958). They can rightly be considered the first peasants of the island. They worked singly or in groups in each other's gardens. In some settlements, each family had its own piece of land, but others would come to help lay it fallow if asked. Because tools like axes and knives were in short supply, they shared the few they had. Their invasions of neighbouring plantations were partly motivated by the need to steal tools from the white planters. To survive in the woods, some maroons became hunters or fishermen and ate wild fruits and animals.

When a slave ran away, he either went alone or with comrades, leaving on the plantation his concubine and his children if he had any. After he had established himself somewhere, he might return to take his family away with him. Dutertre (1667: 536) notes:

As soon as his garden produced something, the husband came to look for his wife and his children, and other maroons came also to bring other slaves with them. No one knows with what abundance fugitive slaves nourished themselves, for they have everything: things that they find in the woods, that they accommodate to their way and their taste. (Dutertre 1667: 536)

Plantation slaves secreted in their huts weapons, axes and other tools that they would give to maroons who came to visit them in the evenings. It was against this practice that the Council of Léogane in 1739 stipulated: 'All weapons, spears, swords, repiers, even the machetes which will be in the said black huts will be confiscated' (Règlement du Conseil de Léogane 1739). This also explains why some slaves who ran away were able to take with them agricultural and hunting tools.

The maroons of Bahoruco exchanged the produce of their gardens first among themselves, then with other neighbouring maroons and finally with Spaniards in a public market in Neybe. Maroons from other parts of Haiti were able to attend unnoticed neighbouring public markets, selling and buying whatever they could. One learns from a report that 'they came to the market in Neybe, bringing the products of their hunting, which they sold to Spaniards from whom they received in exchange weapons, munitions and dry goods' (Archives des Colonies, 1783).

It was also with the object of militarily strengthening their outposts that the maroons of Grand-Bois trade with the Spaniards. 'Maroons of Grand-Bois also sold leathers to Spaniards doubtless for weapons and munitions with which they faced victoriously the attacks in 1774 and 1775' (Archives des Colonies, 1777). Maroons who were not close to Santo Domingo were not able to trade with the Spaniards; in order to acquire weapons, they were forced to make informal arrangements with overseers and plantations slaves.

The Spanish, whose government considered France its enemy, were true accomplices of maroons, providing them with political refuge on their side of the island (Moreau de Saint-Méry 1958). Despite repeated interventions of the local French administration requesting the Spanish government to return slaves for prosecution, their call for extradition fell on deaf ears.

A developed economy did not exist in the maroon communities; it was rather an economy of survival, made so by political circumstances and the necessity for maroons to be on the alert and ready to face armed troops of the colony at any time. The maroons had to take a series of precautions, one of which was not to light fires in daylight so as not to reveal their position. Thus, Dutertre (1667: 537) noted that the colonial administration which sometimes tried to locate the maroon settlements was not always able to do so because the maroons devised to cook only at night so that the smoke would not indicate to outsiders the location of their camp.

OTHER ASPECTS OF SOCIAL LIFE

Their languages reflected the social life of the maroons. African, Creole and Spanish-speaking slaves influenced the formation of Maroon Creole, which was not very different from the Creole spoken on the plantations but which contained a certain number of Spanish words. The majority of maroons spoke Creole, having learned it during their stay on the plantations.

Their mating pattern was also created by the force of historical circumstances. In most maroon settlements, there were more men than women. Among the women who lived there were those captured during maroon raids on the plantations (Arrêté du Conseil de Léogane 1711: 476); there were also a few who came by themselves. Dutertre (1667: 537) mentions the fact that 'black women imitated them [fugitive slaves] and went there with their young children of seven or eight days old.'

Not all maroons had concubines; the most privileged were the leaders, the Voodoo priests and other powerful persons. The shortage of women and the political circumstances did not allow maroons to reproduce themselves the best way they could. However, there were also some exceptions. For example, Moreau de Saint-Méry (1958, III: 1135) noted the presence of older men who had been born in those camps.

Having poor relations with the planters, they could not benefit from the medical care system in the colony: maroons had access neither to the plantations' physicians nor their nurses, but in each camp, there was at least a medicine man. We are told that the maroons of Bahoruco, led by Santyague, were suffering from dysentery, but under the care of a medicine man, most of them regained their health (Moreau de Saint-Méry 1958).

MARRONAGE AND VOODOO

Every attempt at reconstructing the Voodoo religion as practised by maroons can be only conjectural. Voodoo was the only cult available to them in those rural settlements, and theirs was but one 'brand' of Voodoo among the various kinds practised on the plantations. There was evidently an ongoing process of religious syncretism here. Slaves who joined the camps had some experience of Voodoo as practised on the plantations where they had lived, and the maroons themselves participated sporadically in Voodoo ceremonies held on the plantations (see Fouchard 1972: 535–8).

In the maroon settlements, the phenomenon of syncretism took place, for some of them were previously baptised and acculturated in some ways in the emerging Creole culture.[5] In Bahoruco, the first maroons were Indians, and then blacks came to join them. Some Indian traits found in Voodoo, for example the god Zemi, may have come from a syncretism that originated in Bahoruco (Laguerre 1973a).

Moreau de Saint-Méry (1958, II: 1136) reports religious syncretism among the maroons. He writes that Santyague, a Spanish Creole born in Banique, served a long time as bush priest in Bahoruco: 'Santyague, who lived with the maroons for more than fifty years, abusing their superstition, played among them the role of *Padre* (priest). He taught them how to pray in Spanish. A small cross and a rosary were two weapons in his hands with which he took advantage of their weak reason' (Moreau de Saint-Méry 1958, II: 1136).

Although Voodoo was a secret cult on the plantations, it was practised openly in the maroon camps, where Voodoo ceremonies were performed to mark the rites of passage. The fact that they were continually exposed to possible retaliation by the French no doubt motivated the maroons to turn to their Voodoo *loas* (spirits) for protection.

Maroon leaders – the great majority of whom were Voodoo priests – often introduced themselves to slaves as prophets, as authentic representatives and interpreters of the will of the Voodoo *loas* (spirits). Never did they preach the submission of the slaves to the colonists: rather they exhorted them to revolt against their masters and to sabotage their properties, and they incited numberless slaves to leave the plantations and to join the maroon settlements. The underlying idea was that, without political freedom, there could be no possibility for cultural and religious freedom.

Around the second half of the eighteenth century, maroon settlements became the privileged field of retreat for Voodoo priests, recognised as such in the colony. Persecuted by the colonial power for the 'crime' of attempting to poison their masters, those not sent to jail joined the maroons (see Chapter 4). During the earthquake of June 1770, the walls of several prisons collapsed, killing a huge number of prisoners. Among those who survived the disaster were some Voodoo priests, who joined the maroons (Justin 1826: 117).

The leaders' success depended not only on their political rhetoric, but also on their ability to convince slaves that they were executing the desires of the *loas* (spirits). Because of the influence they had on the slaves, the Voodoo priests were all genuine leaders who could incite slaves to engage in revolutionary activities.

In 1757, there appeared the *houngan* (voodoo priest) and guerilla leader Makandal, who set the whole colony trembling and who has left his mark on Voodoo tradition. Makandal was an African from Guinea. Too proud to accept his slave status, he became the leader of a maroon group. As a plantation slave, he had been well respected by his companions because he was known as a Voodoo priest and a medicine man. It did not take him long to impress his followers and convince them of his religious calling, presenting himself as a prophet sent by Voodoo *loas* (spirits):

Makandal predicted the future, he had visions and an exceedingly strong and vigorous eloquence . . . He had persuaded the Blacks that he was immortal and he had instilled in them such terror and such respect that they considered it an honour to serve him on bended knee and to render unto him the worship one owes only to the divinity whose representatives he declared himself to be. The most beautiful black women fought for the honour of sharing his bed. (Archives du Ministère des Colonies, Correspondance Générale, Saint Domingue, 2e serie, C⁹ Carton XXIX; see also Simpson 1970: 235)

Makandal wanted to exterminate the white man from the colony. His decisions were dictated to him (or so the slaves believed) by the *loas* (spirits) whose spokesman he was, and he inspired such fanatical loyalty among the slaves that to refuse to obey Makandal's orders was interpreted by slaves as disobedience to the *loas* he represented.

Makandal's goal was twofold. First, he wanted to unite the blacks by making them politically aware of their slave status. This was going to be a slow process of indoctrination and consciousness raising. Second, he wanted to drive the whites out of the colony, and the success of this struggle evidently depended on unity and solidarity among the slaves. Makandal's plan of battle was very logically thought out, and he did not hesitate to use every means available to achieve his ends. As James (1963: 20–21) points out:

Not only did his band raid and pillage plantations far and wide, but he himself ranged from plantation to plantation to make converts, stimulate his followers and perfect his great plan for the destruction of the white civilisation in San Domingo. An uninstructed mass, feeling its way to revolution usually begins by terrorism and Makandal aimed at delivering his people by means of poison. For six years he built up his organisation, he and his followers poisoning not only whites but disobedient members of their own bands. Then he arranged that on a particular day the water of every house in the capital of the province was to be poisoned and the general attack made on the whites while they were in the convulsions and anguish of death. He had lists of all members of his party in each slave gang; he appointed captains, lieutenants and other officers; he arranged for bands of blacks to leave the town and spread over the plains to massacre the whites.

Debbash (1961) is fully justified in recognising in Makandal the qualified sorcerer-ringleader from whom the masses awaited their liberation. Makandal wanted every slave to accept his plan and put it into action at all levels. Determined to exterminate the colonists, he could not conceive of the fact that any slave would remain neutral and considered mere spectators as traitors to be punished – that is why he did not hesitate to take strong measures against his own fellow slaves who refused to follow his orders.

Despite his vigilance and determination, Makandal was unable to meet his goal. Kidnapped by colonists, he was brought to Cap-Français, where he was publicly burned in 1758. Yet Makandal stayed alive in the minds of the slaves: by lighting the fire of liberation, he inspired others who would come after him to continue the struggle. In the next chapter, I document maroon participation as religious leaders in the revolutionary war for Haitian independence.

SUMMARY

Maroon leaders did not at any moment in their lives in Haiti passively accept the slave system. In their long and heroic resistance, they were able to maintain freedom camps in the mountains that attracted great numbers of slaves year after year. According to Wimpffen (1911: 26), 'the desertion that one calls here *marronage* exists at different degrees in all the plantations.'

These maroons at times terrorised the colonists and were a continual threat to the survival of the colony and to the interests of the colonists. A chronicler of the epoch, Father Margat (1827: 347), writes of these continual maroon raids on the plantations and the troubles that they brought:

> They escape into the woods and the mountains; they hide during the day and at night they come into the neighbouring plantations in order to seize provisions and carry off everything that falls into their hands. Sometimes when they are able to procure weapons for themselves, they assemble during the day, lie in wait and come to attack wayfarers so that we are obliged to send considerable detachments (policemen) to stop their plunder and confine them to their right task.

The Haitian maroon settlements were places of retreat where runaway slaves could discuss and study strategies of attack. They went to the mountains in order to have a base inaccessible to their enemies and to be better able to launch an attack. Maroon desertion was not a simple escape; it was a political exile. Maroons were not spiritually separated from the plantation slaves and urban mulattoes: their political exile was for the sake of better organisation of the movement, so the recourse to and the help of plantation slaves were always judged necessary. The work of liberation was seen as a collective endeavour that had to be plotted out according to the logic of prevailing circumstances in order to find adequate means for an effective use of guerilla tactics. The weekly Voodoo dances, announced by the inviting sound of the drums, were the means for contact, for the development of political consciousness and for exchange of tactics. This strategy of rural guerillas aided by plantation slaves used by maroon leaders of Haiti three centuries ago was later adapted by Mao-Tsé Tung in China, Fidel Castro in Cuba and Che Guevera in South America.

From this discussion of the marronage, we have drawn three conclusions. First, the marronage existed almost everywhere in colonial Haiti and represented a political force as far as the survival of the colony as a colony was concerned. Second, the maroon settlements were self-contained communities, internally structured and a place for the preservation of some African cultural traits and values. Third, Voodoo played a unifying role among maroons and plantation slaves and helped to relieve the psychological stress attached to the dangerous maroon way of life.

4 Revolutionary Voodoo Leaders

It is outside our major interest to trace here the formation of Voodoo as a religion on the island. The dates 1750 and 1767 given for the formation of Voodoo – which are given both by Moreau de Saint-Méry (Paul 1962: 230) and by an anonymous author (Price-Mars 1928: 113) – are misleading because they refer only to the years when colonists became aware of the existence of Voodoo on the island. In this chapter, I present data about revolutionary leaders and their use of Voodoo ideology and Voodoo meetings to show that, by the end of the eighteenth century, colonial Voodoo was indeed a politico-religious movement, and it was a critical factor that – among others – helped make successful the Haitian Revolution.

VOODOO, THE SECRET RELIGION OF THE SLAVES

Despite the hard plantation work to which they were subjected upon their arrival in Haiti, African slaves continued secretly to worship the gods of their ancestors.[1] Certain colonists forced their slaves to worship what the latter considered the god of the whites and forbade them to practise openly their traditional African religions. The god of the whites was interpreted as one who threatened them with chastisement. Many considered the church of the whites as a spectacle – they went to look at some amusing things the priest was doing, but the congregation was denied the possibility of self-expression through dance. In the African religions, dance and communication with the spirits, through a mystical trance in a joyful community, play an important role. Regarding the importance of dance in religious ceremonies in West Africa, Parrinder (1970: 73) writes:

> Dances take place during the weekly and annual festivals. Some of these are simple accompaniments of the music of the drums, but others are traditional and re-enact some event in the mythology and history of the cult. Dancing is done singly and in procession,

and dancers do not normally hold each other. Frequently a spontaneous dance piece may occur under the inspiration of the moment, and the possessed medium gives a message from the god.

This element of feast and of exuberant joy was certainly minimised in the colonists's religion.

Christianity's failure (Courlander and Bastien 1966: 41; Nicholls 1970: 401) to win large numbers of black slaves and to provide them with a satisfactory religious life, and the slaves' passive resistance to the colonists' religion, are two explanations for the rise of Creole Voodoo. The birth of Voodoo as a syncretic religion was partially the result of the slaves' protest against their forced Christianisation and against their assimilation of the whites' values and world. The rise of Voodoo is the testimony, or better still, it is to some extent the expression of the will of slaves to maintain the values of negritude.

Voodoo was the collective memory of the slaves, the means of preservations and perpetuation of their African traditions. The human and physical environment in which religious ceremonies were performed in Africa were evidently not the same in Haiti. The diversity of the slaves' origins made for the richness and diversity of African religious traditions in the creation of Creole Voodoo.

Voodoo played a central role in the slave community in that it furthered a hope for the victory of the slaves' religion over that of the colonists and the total and unconditional liberation of slaves. Confident in the Voodoo *loas* (spirits), slaves were convinced that the result of the battle would determine their future and that of the whites. This faith and hope reinforced their determination for action. Given the circumstances, the decision to worship their *loas* secretly while they continued to go to the official church was also a political tactic. As Bastien remarks, 'Religious co-existence did not exclude resistance on the political plane. The eradication of their social and political organisation did not deter the Africans from trying to regain their freedom' (Courlander and Bastien 1966: 42).

At the beginning of the French colonisation, colonists were not conscious of the political dimension of the slaves' Saturday evening dances. Colonists allowed slaves to dance *Calenda* and *Vaudoux*, which they characterised as erotic and indecent. They could not conceive that those so-called dances were part of the slave's religious practices, and they permitted them because slaves were in better shape to work on the plantations after having danced *Calenda* and *Vaudoux* at the weekend. Those dances that colonists considered as secular were, in part, religious dances: they encouraged group cohesion. In their secret cults, slaves invoked *loas* that their ancestors had worshipped in Africa.

Gradually, colonists became aware of the fact that revolutionary leaders used Voodoo meetings to incite slaves to revolt; then it became necessary to hold these nightly meetings far from the eyes of colonists. They were presided over by known leaders of marronage and attracted many slaves. On Saturday evenings, the ceaseless drums resounded from the woods and indicated the place of meeting. Throughout the colonial era, maroon leaders – as mouthpieces of Voodoo *loas* – preached to participants 'the desertion of slave quarters, the hatred of colonists, the sabotage of plantations, the poisoning of cattle' (Price-Mars 1928: 10). From about 1750, as the colonial administration and the colonists became aware of the revoluntionary ideology furthered by Voodoo and nourished during those secret nightly meetings, they did not hesitate to take strict measures to prevent these meetings, whatever the pretext used (see Moreau de Saint-Méry 1958).

COLONIAL ADMINISTRATION AGAINST VOODOO

In the beginning, the colonists let their slaves dance the *Calenda* whenever a mailboat arrived from France (Moreau de Saint-Méry 1785, V: 234). Colonists would not do the same at the peak of maroon insurrections, for by then they had discovered the relationship between maroon activities and Voodoo meetings, and having discovered the revolutionary ideology disseminated at those nightly meetings, they turned their weapons against them.

Already in 1685, the Black Code in its Article 3 had forbidden all forms of public worship except the Roman Catholic service:

We forbid the public exercise of any other than the Catholic, Apostolic and Roman religion. We will that all persons who act contrary to this prohibition, shall be punished as rebels, and trouble makers. In this view, we forbid all heretical assemblies; declaring the same to be illegal and seditious conventicles, subject to the like punishment, which also shall be inflicted upon those masters who permit their slaves to attend such assemblies. (Peytraud 1897: 159)

Article 16 forbade the assemblies of slaves belonging to different masters:

We likewise forbid slaves, belonging to different masters to assemble together, by night or by day, under pretence or weddings, or any other account, whether it be at the plantation of their master, or any other; or more particularly in any high way, or in unfrequented places; on pain of corporal punishment which at least shall be by whipping and burning on the right shoulder with a red-hot iron, impressed with a *fleur-de-lis*. And, in case of frequent repetition of the same offences, or other aggravating circumstances, they may be punished with death, or according to the discretion of the judges. We enjoin all our subjects, whether officers or others, to pursue the offenders, and to apprehend and conduct them to prison even though no warrant may have been issued against them. (Peytraud 1897: 160)

An ordinance of 1704 forbade slaves 'gathering at night under the pretext of holding collective dances.' An ordinance of 11 January, 1720, renewed the prescriptions of the Black Code against assemblies of slaves (Charlier 1954: 26).

The *Conseil du Cap* promulgated on 11 March 1758, a decree of law forbidding slaves to make *makandals* (representations of 'evil' spells). Also, the *Conseil du Cap* in its meeting on 7 April 1758, forbade slaves and freedmen alike to make, sell, and distribute *garde-corps* (talismans) and makandals. The anonymous author[2] of the *Essai Sur L'Esclavage Et Observations Sur L'Etat Présent Des Colonies*, probably published in 1750, mentions this interdiction that covered the nightly meetings of the slaves:

The dance called water mama and in our colonies *La Mère de l'Eau* (The water mother) is strictly forbidden to them. They make a great mystery of it, and all that is known of it is that it excites very much their imagination. (Cited in Simpson 1970: 234)

Later, Article 3 of the *Arrêt du Règlement du Conseil du Cap*, (18 February, 1761) forbade slaves to gather in the churches between noon and two o'clock and after nightfall. In 1765, a body of policemen, *La Première Légion de Saint-Domingue*, was created for dispersing black gatherings and *Calendas*. Sent to Haiti by Napoléon Bonaparte, Sonthonax, the chairman of the third civil commission – composed of Julien Raimond, Giraud and Leblanc – arrived in Cap on 12 May 1796. He organised in the north 'a rural police charged with eradicating the Voodoo cult' (Sannon 1920, I: 194).

The political dimension of Voodoo – the way it served as a vehicle for a revolutionary ideology – was certainly perceived by colonial administrators. The more they forbade the meetings, the more the slaves flocked to them secretly. Jahn (1958: 520) is right in saying that 'the more the slave owners suppressed and punished the dancers, the dearer, the more sacred did they become to the slaves. The prohibition forced them to secrecy.' The colonists' war against Voodoo was, of course, used by maroon leaders to arouse the slaves against the colonists. As Jahn (1958: 520) writes: 'Their religion became a secret cult, the faithful became sworn brothers, their secret meeting became the cell of the resistance. It needed only an efficient ringleader to drive their angered spirits to rebellion.'

THE USE OF VOODOO IN LIBERATION STRUGGLES

The French chroniclers of the eighteenth century are unanimous in recognising Voodoo's role in the slaves' liberation struggles. They speak of superstitions and also of talismans worn by slaves to make themselves impervious to bullets. Their determination to do away with slavery, their zeal driven to extreme self-sacrifice, can be explained by the slaves' confidence in Voodoo *loas*. Haitian historians and ethnologists – disciples of Price-Mars – have at various times alluded to the kinship between the cult of Voodoo and the zeal of the revolutionaries. Lorimer Denis and François Duvalier (1944: 21) write: 'This is Price-Mars who before the *Société d'Histoire et de Géographie d'Haïti* proclaimed this essential truth: *1804 est issu du Vodou*. The logical process of our thought should make ourselves arrive at the same conclusion' (Denis and Duvalier 1944: 21).

The long experience of slavery taught the slaves that unco-ordinated revolts of individual bands would not expel whites. It was during the nocturnal meetings that they became gradually confident in each other and a solidarity was forged.[3] In the months that preceded the ceremony of Bois-Caiman in 1791, Boukman, a slave of the Plantation Lenormand and a Voodoo priest, made various contacts among chiefs of bands and individual influential slaves – eventually, strategies were communicated to all the slaves.

A well-organised plan had been in the air for a long time, and nothing was left to improvisation. The time for action came – Boukman, in his diplomatic game, had flattered the bourgeois mind of his master Turpin to name him an overseer and a coachman – a position that had put him in continual contact with other slaves. He made friends and succeeded in reviving the political consciousness of the slaves for whom he was responsible, but determined as he was, his influence extended beyond the limits of the Turpin plantation. Having succeeded in convincing his fellow slaves of the necessity of unity for effective action, he decided to organise a mammoth meeting on the night of 14 August 1791. He studied colonial policy closely, patiently awaiting the right moment to call for a general revolt. He studied the reasons why most revolts had not succeeded – especially the great plan of Makandal to exterminate all the whites by poisoning them (see Fouchard 1972).

Boukman knew that such action would lose its meaning and its efficacy if it were not put under the protection of Voodoo *loas* (Mennesson-Rigaud 1958; Rigaud 1953). *Loas* were called upon to make known their will, and a pact was made between the slaves and Voodoo spirits. By coming to supplicate Voodoo *loas* before the opening struggle, the slaves continued an old African tradition. Voodoo *loas* agreed not only to increase their force tenfold, but also to cover their enemies with all sorts of curses.

Circumstances that surrounded the Voodoo ceremony of Bois-Caiman and the ceremony itself are described by an old black slave, Ignace, who lived in one of the plantations of Galliffet. After the plantations of Galliffet were burned Ignace was captured, and he gave this testimony before the court of Cap-Français. His testimony is to some extent corrupted by the colonist Dalmas, who later emigrated to the US and reported Ignace's word in his memoirs. Paraphrasing Ignace's declaration, Dalmas (1814: 117) writes:

> The arrangements of this plan were made a few days before by the principal chiefs, in the Plantation Lenormand, in the Morne-Rouge. Before executing it, they celebrated a sort of feast or a sacrifice, in the middle of a wooden field and not the cultivated plantation of Choiseul, called Le Caiman, where blacks gathered in great numbers. An entirely black pig, surrounded with fetishes and offerings one more whimsical than the others, represented the holocaust to the all powerful genius of the black race. The religious ceremonies that the blacks practised in cutting the throat of it, the avidity with which they drank of its blood, the price that they paid to possess some of its hairs, a kind of talisman, according to them, had to make them invulnerable, characteristic of the African. It was natural that a so ignorant and so wild a race resorted to such frightful crimes, by superstitious rites of an absurd and bloody cult.

Voodoo and Politics in Haiti

This testimony of the epoch is tainted with irony and prejudice. The sacrifice of the pig was a ceremony of blood pacts practised in Dahomey:

> . . . by means of which, the Dahomeans, in a dangerous undertaking, bound themselves to their comrades. Three things are sure to emerge from such pacts: a spirit of solidarity (for better or for worse), unlimited confidence on the part of all who have 'blooded,' and finally complete discretion as regards all secrets imparted under the seal of the blood pact and unfailing punishment of anyone who breaks them. (Métraux 1972: 42)

During the ceremony Boukman, offered to the god of his ancestors this prayer before asking the assembly to fulfill the religious mission of exterminating all the French colonists:

> Bon Dié qui fait soleil qui clairé nou en haut;
> Qui soulevé la mer, qui fait gronder l'orage;
> Bon Dié, zottes tendé, caché nan youn nuage;
> La li gadé nou, li ouè tou ça blan fait;
> Bon Dié blan mandé crime, et pa nous vlé bienfait;
> Mais Dié la qui si bon ordonné nous veangeance;
> Li va conduit bra nou, ba nou assistance;
> Jeté pòtrait Diè blan qui soif dlo nan zies;
> Couté la liberté qui parlé nan coeur nou tous.

> The God who created the sun which gives us light,
> Who rouses the waves and rules the storm,
> Though hidden in the clouds, he watches us.
> He sees all that the white man does.
> The God of the white man inspires him with crime,
> But our God calls upon us to do good works.
> Our God who is good to us orders us to revenge
> our wrongs.
> He will direct our arms and aid us.
> Throw away the symbol of the God of the whites
> Who has so often caused us to weep,
> And listen to the voice of liberty,
> Which speaks in the hearts of us all.
>
> (Sannon 1920, I: 53)

At the end of the ceremony, Boukman told the assembly that the *loas* had agreed to his plan. His words are echoed by the black slave Ignace:

> Time of vengeance has come; tomorrow in the night, all the whites must be killed . . . No more delay, no more fear, the universality of the conjuration does not leave any refuge, any hope of salvation for the whites. All will undergo the same lot; and if some of them avoid our poniards, they will not escape the activity of fire that will reduce the plains in cinders. (Dalmas 1814: 116)

According to Boukman's plan, on the night of the sacrifice, the slaves of Cap-Français were to burn the houses and kill the colonists while the slaves of the plains did the same. It was a question of attacking the colonists on different fronts at the same time in order to create panic and thereby to take control of the situation. Despite all their determination, the slaves did not succeed in taking over the city of Cap-Français – they were forced to give up and move to the plains, where they burned everything that came into their hands. On 24 August 1791, camped in one of the plantations of Galliffet, they addressed the following letter to the governor De Blanchelande: 'It is too late. God (*Gran-Mét*) that struggles for the innocent is our guide. He will never abandon us. So here is our motto: to vanquish or to perish' (Justin 1826: 209).

In this ultimatum sent to De Blanchelande, they took God as their witness. They were fully convinced that God was on their side – this explains their zeal. James (1963: 88) describes the ardour with which they ravaged the beautiful plantations of the north:

> Each slave-gang murdered its masters and burnt the plantation to the ground. The precautions that De Blanchelande had taken saved Le Cap, but the preparation otherwise had been thorough and complete, and in a few days one-half of the famous North Plain was a flaming ruin. From the Cap, the whole horizon was a wall of fire. From this wall continually rose thick black volumes of smoke, through which came tongues of flame leaping to the very sky. For nearly three weeks the people of Le Cap could barely distinguish day from night, while a rain of burning cane straw, driven before the wind like flakes of snow, flew over the city and the shipping in the harbour, threatening both with destruction.

Voodoo had played a major role in the struggle for independence. All the leaders were to some degree affiliated publicly or privately with Voodoo or at least used it for political goals (Madiou 1922).

Made zealous by *houngans* (voodoo priests) and confident in the power of *loas*, slaves went to war joyfully. They were exhorted by their chiefs that, if they did die, they would return to live with their parents in Africa (Mennesson-Rigaud 1958).

The Haitian historian Madiou received from veterans of the war of independence eyewitness accounts of battles and of heroic exploits of the slaves, and this is what gives inestimable value to his writings. According to Madiou (1922), chiefs always wore talismans or some sign of their spirit protectors. He further reports that the guerilla leader Halaou always had sorcerers in his band to give them courage. In their march against the enemy, by the sound of drums, trumpets and *lambis*, sorcerers sang that their leader was invulnerable to bullets. In this band, each slave wore as talisman a tail of an ox that was supposed to stop the enemy's bullets. At the head of 12 000 men, Halaou was received in the capital by Sonthonax. The supreme chief, writes Madiou, 'almost nude, covered with fetishes, holding a chicken on his side, sat near the representative of the French Republic who was covered with tricolor ribbons' (cited in Mennesson-Rigaud 1958: 63).

Revolutionary leaders presented themselves as prophets having a divine mission to fill and as continually listening to *loas* and their decisions as dictated to them by *loas*. Madiou writes:

> Biassou surrounded himself with sorcerers, magicians . . . When the exaltation comes to its peak, Biassou followed by his sorcerers introduced himself to the crowd and revealed that the spirit of God inspired him, he announced to Africans that if they fall in the battle, they would go to revive themselves in their ancient tribe in Africa. Their hideous cries extended far in the woods, songs and somber drums began again, and Biassou taking advantage of those moments of exaltation pushed his band against the enemies that he surprised in the middle of the night. (Cited in Mennesson-Rigaud 1958: 64)

Hyacinthe was only 21 when he became the leader of the guerilla band of Croix-des-Bouquets. He visited plantations and convinced the slaves that he was divinely inspired. Tradition has it that he went to the battlefield, crying: *Boulett cé dlo* (Forward! Forward! The bullets are as dust!) (Sannon 1920, I: 103. See also Simpson 1970: 236). About him, Madiou writes, 'Hyacinthe brandished a tail of ox and defeated the regiments of Artois and of Normandie that shot mercilessly. Hyacinthe revived the courage of his troops, by brandishing his ox tail, facing death fearlessly' (cited in Mennesson-Rigaud 1958: 62).

In the neighbourhood of Léogane, slaves and freedmen had as their chief a mulatto, Romaine-La-Prophétesse (Rigaud 1953: 66; Justin 1826: 62). He claimed to be the godchild of the Virgin Mary, and said that it was at the orders of the Virgin Mary that he killed colonists – he convinced his followers in such a way that nobody dared to contradict him. He always carried on his saddle-horse a *rangé* chicken (one having magical power) as a talisman and went in to battle scoffing at bullets and bayonets.

In February 1792 Colonel Malenfant started to attack a camp of blacks located at Fonds-Parisien in the Plain of Cul-de-Sac. He also mentions the rebels' Voodoo practices.

> As we drew near the camp we were amazed to see huge poles stuck at the side of the road each crowned with a different dead bird, arranged in a different position. Some had herons, some white chickens, others black chickens. In the roadway birds had been chopped up, thrown down at intervals and surrounded by stones artistically arranged; finally we came across seven or eight broken eggs circled by zig-zag lines. (Malenfant 1814: 217)

The revolutionary leader Toussaint Louverture resorted to diplomacy when he was dependent on Bonaparte and well before that when he was a slave on the plantation of the Fathers of Charity of Cap Français. According to oral tradition, he used to practise his ancestors' religion secretly. He was a medicine man, and he used magic in his treatments. His openness toward Christianity was partially a clever political tactic. As Descourtilz (1935: 224) writes:

> Toussaint Louverture, sometimes protector, sometimes violator of temples consecrated to the Eternal, the day when he learned that the French had decided advantages, said to the pastor of Gonaives, holding a cross in his hand: I do not want to serve this God any more. Then crushing it under his feet, with his own sacriligious arm, he began firing at the Church.

Toussaint Louverture worshipped Ogoun Ferraille his Voodoo spirit protector (Rigaud 1953: 67). According to the general belief of his Voodoo followers, Toussaint Louverture's decisions were often dictated to him by his spirit protector.

After Toussaint Louverture's deportation to France, Dessalines replaced him and continued the struggle. Lorimer Denis and François

Duvalier (1944: 26) recount the ceremony of investiture during which Dessalines was elected the supreme chief of the revolution:

> Dessalines, who was designated to drive the armies to the battle, had to be the object of special preparation. Many came to protect him and inspire him: Loco, Petro, Ogoun Ferraille, Brisé Pimba, Caplaou Pimba, Marinette Bois-Chèche, all deities of gunpowder and of fire. First they made him invulnerable for the blood poured out during the ceremony in Bois-Caiman, the fig, symbol of Loco, the powder of Pimba, and of Brisés added to wheat flour were all part of the magical composition that would save Dessalines from bullets.

Dessalines's allegiance to Voodoo is well known. We know how he managed to inspire fanaticism in his troops:

> The Congo blacks and other Guineans were so superstitiously affected by the utterances of Dessalines that they even let him persuade them that to die in battle at the hands of the French was nothing but a blessing, since it meant they were immediately conveyed to Guinea where, once again, they saw Papa Toussaint who was waiting for them to complete the army with which he proposed to reconquer Haiti. This absurd system worked so well, said the informant, everyone went into the attack with supernatural dash, singing the traditional songs of Guinea as though already possessed by hope of seeing old friends once more. (Descourtilz 1935: 383–4)

It was partially confidence in Voodoo *loas*, the political instructions of their followers and the unifying effect of this belief that resulted in the political independence of Haiti. However, Voodoo was not the only factor that explained the success of the Haitian Revolution. Voodoo could not have developed as a politico-religious movement without being supported by other critical factors:

1. The development of sugar plantations, which provoked an increase in the black population (blacks outnumbering whites greatly), obviously made African religions more significant culturally and politically.
2. The tremendous increase in the black population caused an increase in the population of maroon settlements. The maroons helped cause the revolution of 1791–1803.
3. Events in France also had their aftermath in the colony – the

French Revolution did have a great bearing on the movement in Haiti. In fact, it was a critical factor in the success of the slave revolt: the events in France did not necessarily cause Boukman's uprising, but they did paralyse the colonial regime's ability to deal with the revolt.

4. The non-hostility of Spaniards toward Haitian slaves partially explains the success of the maroons' guerilla tactics. The slaves knew they could escape to Santo Domingo at any time without risking being sent back to Haiti.

5. Other factors – such as the alliance of blacks and mulattoes, racial relations and class structures – also had their bearing on the Haitian Revolution.

CONCLUSION

Religion was one among other variables that explain the success of the Haitian Revolution. Everywhere in the New World blacks resisted slavery by committing suicide, killing colonists, performing abortions, establishing maroon communities and periodically organising revolts. Everywhere in the New World religion, to a certain extent, played a role in the blacks' struggle to liberate themselves from the colonial regime. The uniqueness of the Haitian case resides not in the blacks' opposition to colonial powers, nor in the use of religion for political goals, but in its successful result.

As a result of the sugar revolution, the colony passed from a subsistence to an export economy. The sugar revolution made Haiti, during the second half of the eighteenth century, the wealthiest colony of France. More blacks were brought to the island to work on the plantations. However, more preoccupied with making great profits than with maintaining the racial balance, the colonists allowed the black population to outnumber the white. The multiplication of large sugar cane plantations caused the concentration of blacks on some plantations in the northern part of Haiti.

The sugar revolution created a new matrix upon which new patterns of race relations were shaped. If in the beginning colonists were not primarily concerned with distancing themselves from the mulatto and black population, it was not any more so by the time of the sugar revolution. The passage from small property holdings to large sugar plantations provoked more acute social discrimination at the expense of blacks and mulattoes. By using force and by manipulating the law, colonists oppressed both blacks and mulattoes, making them unable to occupy key political positions.

Although maroon communities existed from the beginning, the black demographic revolution made it difficult for colonists to watch over maroon activities. The size and number of these communities increased, and the maroons' eventual chance of fleeing to Santo Domingo or elsewhere made their presence a danger to the survival of the colony. The maroons – initiators of the black power movement – developed guerilla warfare expertise throughout the eighteenth century.

The sugar revolution also had a bearing on black family structures. To survive, the existing black families developed strategies. Because they could not perpetuate their African ways of life and were not inclined to adopt the offical monogamy recognised by law, they adapted themselves in various ways, depending on the social atmosphere of the plantations on which they worked, the demographic balance (sex ratio), the social and economic status of slaves within the slave community and other factors related to the ecological niching as a whole. Where black families (or households) existed, they served as the base for secret Voodoo cults. The household was the privileged place where slaves worshipped their *loas* protectors.

The structure of slave society, the problems the clergy had to face in the Christianisation of slaves, the kind of priests sent to the island and some resistance to religious assimilation from certain slaves are some of the factors that explain the partial failure of Christianity in colonial Haiti. Christianity was perceived as the whites' religion and the defender of the whites' interests – more as magic than as religion. Voodooists used it to complement the magical power inherent in Voodoo.

The differences in slave populations and ecological niches made possible the rise of various Creolised cults – with time, each Voodoo centre developed its own tradition. Even when historical circumstances demanded greater solidarity among blacks, Voodoo cults had not reached any type of ritual uniformity.

Although other variables – such as the fact that the French Revolution paralysed the French regime's dealings with the revolutionary blacks of Haiti and the existence of the black–mulatto coalition – must be considered, Voodoo played a very important role in the Haitian Revolution as far as it allowed the unification of slaves and provided them with a revolutionary ideology.

The nightly meetings that resulted in the formation of Voodoo were banished as soon as the colonists saw the relationship between them, marronage and periodic slave revolts. The more the meetings were prohibited and the participants persecuted, the more secret they became and the more the slaves felt a link of solidarity through them.

During those so-called 'Saturday evening dances', slaves fulfilled their obligation toward the gods of their ancestors and were imbued with African traditions. Besides religious songs and rites, there were also intensely political songs which were meant to nurture their feelings against slavery and to incite them to revolt. Colonists were aware of what happened in those meetings, for one of them, Drouin de Bercy, reports a refrain that slaves usually sang during their initiation rites:

> *Aia, bombaia, bombé,*
> *Lamma Samana quana,*
> *E van vanta,*
> *Van docki.*

> We swear to destroy the whites
> And all that they possess;
> Let us die
> Rather than fail to keep this vow.
> (Drouin de Bercy 1814: 178)

The part played by Voodoo priests in the struggles for independence has been amply documented. All those who periodically took the leadership of slave bands presented themselves as prophets in continual touch with Voodoo *loas*. Well-known priests always succeeded in gathering unity around their person and in driving bands to revolutionary activities. As Debbash (1961: 95) remarks, 'The revolt of Haiti cannot be explained without conferences that gathered the plantation slaves around the sorcerers.'

Voodoo as practised by slaves was not escapism. It was not meant to make the slaves forget their condition but served as a focus for the development of political consciousness. It was used to prepare people for the liberation struggles, and because it represented the slaves' interests, it developed the cohesion and the unity of the masses.

The interdictions imposed on black meetings were interpreted by the Voodooist mass as an open attack against the *loas*, their protectors. Prophets arose and stated their goals as attempts to save the interests of African *loas*. They claimed to be their messengers. The liberation of 'the cultural', of 'the religious' elements of their life (to allow slaves to serve the *loas* of their ancestors) could be achieved only through political liberation. But because the system was too oppressive to allow slaves to express their political determination, they used religion as their last plank of salvation to start political liberation. It was a question of recovering 'the political' by recovering first 'the religious'. Organised Voodoo became for the slaves the basis for a political recouping of the culturally religious: it was there as a major aspect of the struggles.

It is impossible to understand colonial Voodoo without seeing its political kinship to the demands of the masses. Voodoo was for the slaves a language, a way of expressing and of resisting their cultural and religious assimilation. It was the collective memory of slaves, as far as it preserved and perpetuated the African religious traditions. It was the focus for the development of political consciousness so far as it allowed the slaves to be aware that their values were different from those of the whites and also as far as it allowed them to express their negritude. It was the centre of appreciation of black and emergent Creole values, so far as it allowed them to distinguish these from European values.

If the struggle for independence was not a religious war in the manner of medieval crusades, it is still true that Voodoo was never absent from the battlefield. The slaves' desire to maintain their African traditions and the war of colonists against the centre of their culture drove them to a political struggle. The singularity of the Haitian Revolution stays in part in the religious ardour of the slaves, inflamed by the leaders, who in turn were inspired by Voodoo *loas* to exterminate the colonists of Haiti. Revolutionary leaders successfully used Voodoo to make Haiti the first black republic in the New World and the second nation to achieve independence in the western hemisphere and to make the Haitian Revolution the first social revolution in the Third World.

5 Secret Societies

Secret societies have been widespread in Haiti ever since the country's independence from France in 1804. Each one is part of a network and serves as an underground government, police force and judicial body. The extent of their control over rural Haiti has not yet been evaluated. Their importance in regard to rural politics cannot be ignored. The focus of this chapter is on one kind of secret society – the Bizango – because it has ramifications all over the island. There is another kind, found especially on the island of La Gonâve, where the secret society is also an agricultural association. However the functioning of the latter as well as that of other secret societies will not be analysed here.

Bizango operates in the northern, western, southern and central portions of Haiti. It takes its name from one of the African tribes from the Bissagot Islands whose members were brought to colonial Haiti for plantation work (Moreau de Saint-Méry 1958: 49). The Bissagot Islands, an archipelago of five islands, are located off the Coast of Kakonda, between Sierra Leone and Cape Verde. Referring to slaves coming from the Bissagot Islands, Moreau de Saint-Méry (1958: 49) writes, 'these blacks are good hunters and sure guardians of living quarters in the plantations.' The participation of Bissagot slaves in the formation of maroon communities has already been acknowledged (Debbash 1961; Laguerre 1973a; Debien 1966). However, the reasons why a secret society was named after a particular tribe have yet to be fully explained. The concentration of slaves of the same ethnic origins in the same region or the leadership role played in a secret organisation by a slave whose ethnic identity was known are two of the main reasons that might explain this identification. It happened sometimes that slave leaders in colonial Haiti gave their names to organisations they formed: there are a few examples of such cases throughout the history of the island. Don Pedro, a maroon, bestowed his name on the Petro cult group that he founded (Métraux 1972). Makandal, a rebel who organised slave revolts in the northern plantations, has also left his name to the Makandal society, which is based in the north (Fouchard 1972). The Mandingue secret society – Mandingue is the name of an African tribe – still has a strong association with the Valley of Artibonite (Peters 1965). Other secret societies such as San Manman, Zobop,

71

Vlinbinding, and San Poèl, which function in the west, carry names
of Creole origin (Courlander 1960: 167).

During the French colonisation of Haiti (1625–1791) maroons
and slave rebels constituted a constant threat to the local French
establishment or administration (Manigat 1977). They were revolutionary slaves who used a large range of strategies and tactics in their
day-to-day resistance to slavery. In more specific terms, the maroon
can be defined as:

> . . . the fugitive slave who has broken with the social order of the
> plantation to live, actually free, but as an outlaw, in areas (generally
> in the woods or in the mountains) where he could escape the
> control of the colonial power and the plantocratic establishment.
>
> The first element in this definition is the existence of a social
> organisation (the plantation system) with a structure and laws,
> within which the servile condition is set down, and with which the
> maroon breaks by fleeing. . . The second element is the possibility
> of taking refuge in a space not actually controlled by the ruling
> authorities and their repressive forces, so that he can escape from
> the hold of the centre by putting himself on the periphery, in a
> marginal but independent situation. . . The third element is the
> insecurity of his new life. . . It is a material, psychological and
> political insecurity. To resist and survive means a psychology of
> risk-taking and a determination to brave adversity and face danger
> . . . The fourth element comes from the necessity to survive by his
> own means. The three main problems of survival are food, shelter
> and defense. (Manigat 1977: 421–2)

In colonial Haiti, there were three types of maroons: urban, rural,
and nomadic (Laguerre 1973a). Colonial maroons were all slaves
who had fled from the plantations in search of freedom. Both rural
and urban maroons established maroon communities with genuine
political, economic and religious systems of their own: nomadic
maroons wandered in streets and rural roads begging and stealing
from plantations whatever they could find. Maroon settlements,
placed in mountainous areas difficult of access to colonists, served as
training grounds for guerilla warfare.

In this chapter I argue that, after the independence of Haiti in
1804, cells of maroon communities have continued to exist through
the formation of secret societies. Secret societies are thus seen as the
channels that the 'maroons' of contemporary Haiti use to protect
their personal interests and those of their own communities. Colonial

maroons fought against the slave system and all its evil forces; this was a racial war, a fight against the French planters. In contemporary Haiti, maroons who constitute the membership of secret societies continue to fight – although not against white people. They still stand strong to keep safe the boundaries of power of their local communities and to prevent other groups of people from threatening their communities.

Simmel (1950: 346) distinguishes two types of secret society: in one, the formation of the group itself is concealed while in the other, 'the formation of the group is completely known, while the membership, the purpose, or the specific rules of the association remain secret.' The Bizango secret society belongs to the latter type, for its existence is known not only to people who hold membership in it but also to outsiders – because Bizango people walk in groups in the streets at night, one may be able to encounter a group and find out who they are.

Information on the Bizango secret society was given to me by informants who were invited to join the association and who, later on, converted to Protestantism. These informants live in the Artibonite Valley and the central plateau of Haiti. They were willing to talk about the functioning of the association, but not to reveal secret languages, strict rules or individual members' names. One informant has even allowed me to have a slide showing a Bizango passport that he used to carry with him at night for protection from other rival secret societies.

THE FUNCTIONING OF A SECRET SOCIETY

The importance of secrecy in the formation and functioning of secret societies cannot be overestimated. For Simmel (1950: 345), 'the secret determines the reciprocal relations among those who share it in common.' Secrecy is the principle at the base of the formation of such groups – however, secrecy cannot be maintained without the proper initiation and training of neophytes. Initiation and training are specific moments when one learns the rules of the game. An initial training is not enough for one to become a full member; cyclical rituals must be performed to strengthen linkages among members, obedience to the leaders, and faithfulness to the purposes of the secret society.

Not everyone can become a member of the Bizango society – one must be invited by a member to do so. The acceptance of such an invitation, however, does not make one immediately eligible to be briefed on all the rules of the secret society. These rules are revealed step by step to the newcomer as the person is being tested in other ways.

The recruitment process is done through a kind of selective and elective brotherhood. The initiation ritual – consisting of recruitment, participation in formal rituals and teaching the society rules – is a way of integrating newcomers to the group. To maintain the unity of the society as one body, other rituals are also performed.

Mackenzie (1967: 13) has mentioned the following variables as characteristics of a secret society: 'the initial ritual, the ordeal, the oath, the myth or legend that supports the secrecy and the segregation of men from women.' The Bizango society will be described here in the light of these characteristics.

The Bizango society has over the years developed its own Voodoo tradition. During the colonial era, Bizango was the spirit protector of Bissagot slaves – he is still known in Voodoo mythology as a warrior and a violent spirit. Bizango mythology is not well known in Haitian literature, however, because of the secrecy to which the members of the society are bound.

Members of the Bizango society, as well as other Voodooists, believe that the universe is governed by weak and strong spirits. Some of them are of African origin; others are Creoles, that is, born in the New World. Bizango belongs to the family of strong spirits, born in time immemorial in Africa, and his function in Voodoo mythology is to protect the interests of his followers. The main reason for his protection is to return them to Africa when they die so that they may live in the land where he resides.

In the context of Haitian peasantry, a belief in Bizango means that the peasant feels assured of protection against individuals who may try to rob him of his land, and a guarantee that he will return to live in Africa after death. These two elements serve as the practical and eschatological base from which they operate.

The first phase in the educational process by which one becomes a member of a secret society is the 'initial ritual.' During this ritual of initiation, the individual learns about the peculiar belief system that serves as the philosophical basis for the existence of the group. As mentioned earlier, this philosophy, which presents Voodoo spirits as guardians of peasant lands, is a combination of peasant political thought and Voodoo belief. While going through the initiation phase, the individual also becomes aware of the identity of others who belong to the group, as well as of the group stratification, the function of each individual, and the existence of competing groups in the district or elsewhere on the island. The individual is also admonished about the importance of secrecy for the survival of the society, the role that he will play in the association, and the financial contribution (monthly fees) that he will be called upon to give. Moreover, the neophyte is invited to attend meetings for an entire year before he can be accepted as a full member. During this probation period, he is also called to perform what might be considered by Haitian standards 'dirty tasks,' for example, cleaning another's outhouse.

The novice must be tested on certain grounds before the elders can decide whether to accept his request to join the society. They must find out through various trials if the individual can keep the secrets of the group. As happens also in other secret societies, 'the novice is treated as a stranger, a spy, an alien, or some other outsider, who must submit to various tests' (Mackenzie 1967: 17). To assess a novice's ability to keep a secret, elders may send individuals who do not belong to the group to check up on him, to see if he seems likely to reveal to others what has been said and done in group meetings – he may even be tempted to do so for a woman's favour or for financial reward.

When the elders accept someone as a permanent member of the group, a ceremony, pervaded with the atmosphere of magic, is held. The role of such a ceremony, which is not peculiar to this Voodoo secret society, is 'to impress the candidate with the seriousness of the step he is about to take' (Hobsbawm 1959: 151). During such a ceremony, the rules of the association are clearly explained to the individual and the names of other members are revealed to him. At the same time, they make sure that he understands what might happen to him if he decides to leave the society, or reveal its secrets and the names of individual members to outsiders.

The candidate must also make a speech explaining that he is ready to join the association, and that he agrees not to reveal to anyone its secrets or the names of its members. To ratify his agreement, the candidate is invited to drink some pig blood from a cup that is presented to him. This is a kind of oath that binds the individual to the group.

Like other secret societies, the Bizango association holds periodic meetings 'to reaffirm the unity of the members' (Hobsbawm 1959: 152). Once a month, they organise a night-time march or rally and once a week, they meet for a couple of hours to worship together, during which time a member may be possessed by Bizango, the spirit-patron of the association.

The Bizango society has such 'ritual furnishings' as banners, flags, passports and uniforms. Banners and flags are black and red – these were the colours of the Haitian national flag during the Duvalier era, symbolising the solidarity that must exist between blacks and mulattoes in the case of eventual threats by the nation's enemies. Members of the Bizango society were black trousers or skirts and red shirts or blouses with a black cross drawn on the back of the shirt or the blouse.

At night every member of the Bizango society must carry with him a special passport for protection against members of other rival secret societies. Secret societies compete against one another for power, for by becoming powerful, they may attract many followers to the Voodoo temple to which they belong, and in so doing, they may come to exert control over an entire district.

The Bizango passport is a sheet of paper with a stamp on its upper left corner – such a paper can be bought from the *Bureau des Contributions* (tax office). On its borders, there are coloured lines that are the same as the colours of the society's flag. On that sheet of paper, there is a prayer – then the passwords and the names of villages and secret society leaders that have agreed to acknowledge such a passport.[1] In the middle of the passport stands a black and red cross. Individuals who go out at night without a passport may be admonished by secret society members not to do so again, or if they must walk at night, may be invited to join the association. A few cases have been reported of individuals being beaten up at night by their enemies who happened to be members of the Bizango society. However, the Bizango secret society can by no means be considered a criminal association.[2]

EVENING RALLIES

Evening rallies are rituals performed monthly by the society to strengthen the unity of the group. Drumming and the use of a conch (*lambi*) signal to the members that the association is about to hold a meeting. Both men and women take part in these rallies, and the members gather in the Voodoo temple before they start a procession in which they carry with them flags and banners.

Before leaving their temple to start the march, marchers admonish neighbours through songs not to talk about what they might see or hear. Voodoo temples are sometimes so close to surrounding houses that, when they are having a meeting, neighbours cannot help but be aware of what is going on. If they are awake at night, they can hear songs sung by the society and recognise the voices of some members. This following song invites neighbours not to reveal anyone's identity:

> *La fanmi bizango io pinga diol nou*
> *La fanmi io pinga bouch nou*
> *Moin mété ion band bizango asouè ia déiò*
> *Nou levé matin na palé ki jan mtap dansé*
> *Pinga diol nou.*

Neighbours and friends of the Bizango society,
Be careful about what you might say.
When we organise a Bizango rally,
We don't wish for you to start talking about our
songs and dances, the morning after.

After they have sung this song, Legba, a Voodoo spirit – the guardian of gates and crossroads – is invoked. He is called to open the gates so that the people can leave the temple, and he is supposed to protect them as they walk through the streets at night.

> *Ouvè, ouvè*
> *Mdi ouvè chemin*
> *Papa Legba, o*
> *Société an la ki rantré.*

Open, open
We say, open the gates
Papa Legba
The society is ready to leave the temple.

When the society is out walking in the streets there is a specific order that members follow. Leading the band is the *sentinelle* (guard), followed at a distance by the major (*lansé*) with a rope in his hands, and behind him walks a *porteur* (carrier) who carries a small coffin (*sèkèy madoulè*). The *porteur* is accompanied by two to four flag carriers, who are usually women; then comes the crowd and finally the leader of the band with his bodyguards. The coffin contains the common funds of the society. Once a month, the faithful are called on to contribute to these funds.

If the society meets a passerby, it is the duty of the *sentinelle* to stop that person. The major passes the rope around his neck, and the flag carriers gather round him to identify him for the crowd. The *sentinelle* puts his hands on him and waits for the leader of the band to come forward. When the entire crowd is assembled, the leader asks to see the passerby's passport, or may start asking questions to find out if he has any friend or relative who belongs to the Bizango society – or indeed if he belongs to another friendly secret society or Voodoo group. If he proclaims himself a Voodooist, the leader starts shaking hands with him to discover the extent of his Voodoo knowledge. The Bizango handshake is a ritual and a means of communication. Bizango members refer to it as a secret language. The preliminary phase of the Bizango handshake begins in this way: first the group leader puts his index finger in the upper palm of the right hand of the other person and presses his index finger on the person's skin so that he becomes aware of the sign. This is a greeting sign by which people reveal their identity to each other. Second, they shift from right to left hand and to right hand again in a way that only a degree holder Voodooist [a ranking member of the Voodoo church] can decode.

Some members of the Bizango secret society carry a machete round their waist at night to defend themselves should they meet a rival band. This is more of a ritual than anything else as a band has power only over a certain delineated domain (a village, a rural or urban district) and the society would not try to operate in someone else's domain. While walking at night in the streets, Bizango members sing this song:

> *Li minuit o li lè pou malé*
> *Banm pasé*
> *Li minuit o li le pou malé*
> *Map volé*
> *Mgin devan Baron pou mal dansé*
> *Li minuit o li lè pou malé.*

> It is mid-night, it is time for us to leave
> let us go
> It is mid-might, it is time for us to leave
> Let us fly
> We have to go to the cemetery and dance for

Baron Samedi.
It is mid-night, let us go.

During their initiation, members of the Bizango society receive training in guerilla warfare tactics to prepare them for the defence of their land against the mulatto and black elite. When they are walking at night, the *sentinelle* can alert the rest of the group at any time, and he routinely does so – for example, when a car or truck is coming their way. He blows his whistle, and the people immediately lie down on both sides of the road or the street so that the driver and passengers of the car cannot see or identify members of the group.

The Bizango secret society begins its rallies after 11 p.m. and returns to the temple at about 3 a.m. These evening rallies are a kind of festive celebration in which people eat, drink, dance and generally enjoy themselves. During Lent members of the secret societies organise rural carnival bands [known as *Rara*] that circulate at night in the countryside.

FROM MAROON COMMUNITIES TO BIZANGO SECRET SOCIETY

Maroon communities in colonial Haiti were formed and functioned on the basis of secrecy. Secrecy was important in order to prevent French colonists from knowing where these communities were located, who the maroons were and what political and economic systems they used to survive (Debbash 1961). Newly arrived maroons were evidently forced to take an oath not to reveal the secret of the community and consequently had to pledge allegiance to the group and obedience to its leaders.

Secrecy was further necessary to facilitate evening raids on the plantations. Passwords were needed for communication between accomplice plantation slaves and maroons[3] – Voodoo provided a basis of solidarity between slaves and maroons in that they were all Voodoo believers (Laguerre 1973b, 1974a, 1974b). Passwords and handshakes helped distinguish friends from spies: secret languages – still used today among Voodooists – were a means to differentiate maroons and Voodooists from outsiders. Passwords, handshakes and secret languages helped to develop and to strengthen a spirit of solidarity among maroons and slaves so that they could fight in their own domains against the brutality of the slave system.

Maroon communities were not homogeneous. Subgroups existed and were formed on the basis of the tribal language spoken by their members and various Voodoo priests and medicine men. Religion was indeed a factor of cohesion and group integration in maroon communities (Laguerre 1973b), and maroon priests played a very important leadership role during the wars for the independence of Haiti. Post-independence secret societies emerged out of subgroups centred on the leadership of Voodoo leaders.

The Bizango society emerged out of maroon communities, and it is not totally a post-independence creation. Marronage offered proper means for the restructuring of groups of slaves who had fled from the plantations, and provided the mechanism by which secret societies could function in colonial Haiti.

After independence, the migration of maroons to cities and valleys – taking over white people's properties – gave rise to the development and maintenance of secret societies. This time the new maroons had to be able to fight back if the French returned, but they also stood in opposition to the black and mulatto elite who failed to provide enough land for the peasants or were indeed trying to take land from them. It was the custom, after independence, for presidents to give large portions of so-called government land to army officers (Nau and Telhomme 1930: 36), and it has been common throughout the history of Haiti for politicians to dispossess peasants of their land. With the agrarian reform initiated by Jean Jacques Dessalines, the first ruler of Haiti (1804–1806), peasants were given enough land for their economic subsistence. Over the years, these lands have been divided and passed from one generation to the next without individuals having ownership papers. Influential politicians often try to take these properties from the peasants, and sometimes are successful in so doing; at other times they are not, meeting with stiff resistance from secret society groups.

Following independence, secret societies – comprising both male and female members – functioned to keep hold of their lands. The *lakou* system was in the process of expansion, and membership of a secret society was a force to resist outsiders' intrusion on one's land and domain. Secret societies created villages and *lakous* solidarity against outsiders and defined the power boundaries of villages.

Networks of secret societies became well known when peasants rose against the Haitian governmental system and the U.S. marines through the Piquets and Kakos revolts (Pierre-Charles 1967: 41).[4] Their association grew out of secrecy because of historic urges to organise group resistance. During the US occupation of Haiti (1915–1934), groups of secret society members pledged their allegiance to the self-proclaimed revolutionary leader, Charlemagne Péralte, and fought against the marines.

Since the US occupation of Haiti, secret societies have continued to function as the hard core section of some Voodoo temples, charged with protecting their districts – as well as the Voodoo temple and congregation to which they belong – against the interference of neighbouring secret societies. Whereas the Voodoo temple is a separate institution to which a secret society may be connected, the Voodoo priest is a kind of public relations man between the outside world and the members of the secret society. Of all the members of a secret society, he is the only one who might be known in that capacity by the general public.

CONCLUSION

The Bizango secret society is a remnant of Haiti's colonial heritage and stands as an integrated unit in the Haitian social structure. Individuals are integrated into such a unit through a ritual of rebirth (ritual of initiation) which every member must undergo, through making an oath of allegiance to the group and through sharing secret languages (handshakes, passwords). The Bizango secret society stands as the conscience of certain districts in Haiti in that it protects the residents against exploitation by outsiders.

The study of secret societies is one way to understand the make up of Haitian society – they are widespread on the island. If such secret societies could establish links making them nodes in a complex network, they would stand as a strong underground government, capable of challenging the Haitian government. However, because of local rivalries, they have not been able to form such a network of relationships.

6 Pilgrimage, Voodoo and Politics

The study of pilgrimage as a socio-religious phenomenon can be carried out at three different levels: (1) the study of shrines as sacred places, (2) the pilgrims themselves, and (3) the goals, motivations and reasons why pilgrims journey to specific shrines in an attempt to gain material and spiritual reward (Raphael 1974: 11; Turner 1974, Turner and Turner, 1978). Pilgrimage as an individual and collective march to a sacred place can be a mechanism for social integration in the same way that Durkheim (1915) perceives the function of religion in society. But religion has also been shown sometimes to play a disruptive role in society, as in the case of nativistic and revitalisation movements (Lanternari 1963; Wallace 1956).

In this chapter, pilgrimage as a social system will be interpreted in terms of a centre-periphery framework. A centre becomes a centre when it is in dialectical relation with a periphery (Galtung 1972; Shils 1974). It is postulated here that because they live in a peripheral situation (not necessarily a geographical, but a spiritual periphery), pilgrims initiate their journeys to shrines to be a part of a spiritual centre. This might be done as a rite of re-affirmation of their faith and purification (Turner 1973). The shrine where Haitian pilgrims congregate will be considered a centre, a 'sacred place,' a focus of spiritual energy, a place of 'hierophany,' where the manifestation of a saint – in this case, the Holy Virgin – has been recorded. In other words, a shrine is a centre in the sense that the 'sacred' is somehow 'located' there and because the pilgrims believe that to be so. Their recognition of a shrine as a spiritual centre is based on their faith and their acceptance of physical healing occurring within and outside the shrine as a gesture of a divine manifestation. Moreover, a shrine as a centre might also be a national symbol, capable of lending force to a nationalist ideology that political activists can at times use for political purposes, as in the case of the Nuestra Señora de Guadalupe shrine in Mexico (Wolf 1958).

In order to describe and explain the social function of the Haitian pilgrimage to the shrine of Notre Dame de Saut D'Eau, I will focus on the one hand on the shrine itself, on the pilgrims before and during their pilgrimage, and on syncretistic processes embracing folk

Christianity and Voodoo practices. On the other hand, I will discuss how Haitian politicians have twice exploited the apparitions of the Holy Virgin in Saut D'Eau in times of national political crisis to make peasants fight against foreign enemies, and also how the pilgrimage plays an integrative role in maintaining the status quo in contemporary Haiti.

The study of pilgrimage is in the process of becoming a specialised field of investigation amongst social scientists researching Latin American societies and cultures. Indeed, a growing body of literature on pilgrimage as a sociological phenomenon is now available (Mair 1959; Gottlieb 1970, Macklin 1973). Religious pilgrimages cannot be considered isolated facts in the national life of Latin American peasants; they are in the very centre of some Latin American religious traditions. Most Latin American countries have their own national and regional shrines, and pilgrimages have special social functions among the peasant population. In these countries every year at certain periods, pilgrims travel to shrines – often far from their homes – to fulfil vows or accomplish other objectives. For example, many Mexicans make their pilgrimage annually to the shrine of Nuestra Señora de Guadalupe, Chileans to Nuestra Señora de Andacallo, Colombians journey to Virgen de Las Lajas, Ecuadorians to the Virgen del Quinche and Virgen del Cisne and Bolivans to Nuestra Señora de Copacabana. Peruvians make their pilgrimage to the Nuestra Señora del Pachacamac shrine, Brazilians journey to the Bom Jesus da Lapa and Dominicans go to Nuestra Señora de Altagracia del Higuey. In Haiti, at the Notre Dame du Mont Carmel or Vierge de Saut D'Eau shrine, the celebration of the feast is on 16 July, the day of the first apparition of the Holy Virgin in Saut D'Eau, a village in western Haiti. On this day the shrine attracts people from the entire island.

There are few ethnographic descriptions of Saut D'Eau pilgrims. Writing early this century, Antoine Innocent (1906: 60–105) gave a good account of the social and religious atmosphere of Saut D'Eau during the month preceding the feast of Our Lady of Mount Carmel. During this month, peasants from all over Haiti converged on Saut D'Eau, travelling by donkey, mule and horse, praying during the journey for their inward conversion and transformation. During this same period, Aubin (1910: 53) was struck by the number of pilgrims who wore *sac collet* (penitential uniforms).

Later, Price-Mars (1928: 168–77) collected from oral traditions the history of the apparitions and of the pilgrimage and provides a description of the Saut D'Eau milieu in July 1926, when he attended the pilgrimage. According to Price-Mars, among the pilgrims there were peasants, Voodooists, prostitutes, beggars, gamblers and penitents. Like Price-Mars, Herskovits (1971: 285–289) recorded his observations on Saut D'Eau while he was there in 1934 and witnessed spirit possession among Voodoo pilgrims.

Alfred Métraux (1957: 92–5) pointed out the continuing Voodooisation of the pilgrimage centre and the huge number of Voodoo priests and pilgrims who visited Saut D'Eau annually. More recently, Hérold Désil – a native of Saut D'Eau – wrote his MA thesis on the ethno-sociology of the Saudolese community. Although his thesis lacks a theoretical framework, Désil gave some original information from his own observations on the economy and the demographic balance of Saut D'Eau and also mentioned the total disappearance of the *feux de la Saint Jean*, which used to take place on the eve of Our Lady of Mount Carmel feast (Désil 1967: 32).

THE VILLAGE

Saut D'Eau, a small village in the *Département* of the west, is situated in the western portion of the Chaine-des-Matheux between Mirebalais and Saint Marc.[1] The village is geographically limited according to a presidential decree of 26 January 1911, as follows: to the east by the *Habitation Louisia*, to the north by the *Habitation Tibreuil*, to the west by the *Habitation Rinville*, and to the south by the *Habitation Lavoute* (Moniteur du 26 janvier 1911). The sergeant commanding the military post, the tax collector, the Catholic priest and a few Voodoo priests are the most influential people in the village.

According to the census of 1950, the village then had a population of about 150 households, that is, about 1314 inhabitants. A more recent census (1971) gave the following figures for Saut D'Eau: 775 houses, 442 families, and 1886 inhabitants. Saudolese villagers – artisans included – hold small farms in nearby Saut D'Eau, where some grow crops for local consumption. As a consequence of the division of the land among inheritors, no large plantations exist in the area. Since the first agrarian reform initiated in 1805 by Jean Jacques Dessalines, the land has been fragmented into small portions and distributed amongst peasants. The Saudolese people are involved mainly in agriculture and live on a subsistence economy base. There are no industries and no factories in Saut D'Eau; foreign business has no investments there.

The public market is held twice a week in the village. Saudolese attend this market to sell the produce from their small farms and to buy what they are in need of. Middlemen buy from market sellers at low prices the goods they can then resell to export companies in Port-au-Prince. The presence of pilgrims in Saut D'Eau during the time of the pilgrimage means that the local market is attended by greater numbers of people, and the village economy improves slightly.

When the annual pilgrimage is over, Saut D'Eau becomes again a quiet place not much different from other Haitian villages. Parents in Saut D'Eau, as elsewhere in Haiti, make great sacrifices to send their children to finish their high school education in Port-au-Prince, the economic centre of the nation. Generally, after graduation, these students do not return to live in the village, looking instead, for jobs in the capital or moving to New York to join relatives. Since the 1960s, owing to harassment by Duvalier's secret police, the emigration of Saudolese to New York has been increasing – furthermore the village faces the problem of the emigration of its active and educated population. With a growing number of emigrants leaving Saut D'Eau, the subsistence economy of the remaining villagers depends more and more upon the money sent by relatives working in Canada and the US.

A few pilgrims also visit Saut D'Eau during Holy Week and for the feast of Notre Dame de la Merci on 24 September. These two feasts do not generate a national migration to the village; rather, the pilgrims come from neighbouring villages. They are few in number and stay in Saut D'Eau for only one or two days – their presence during those times affects the economy and the social life of the village very little.

In Saut D'Eau, as in most of the other Haitian villages, there are neither hotels nor motels. From June onwards, the Saudolese build a few temporary shacks to rent to pilgrims, mainly to vendors. During this period, the cost of renting single rooms increases and it is difficult to find a place to stay if one does not have friends and relatives there. Most of the Saudolese rent a room or two of their homes to pilgrims. Patios and porches are also transformed into rented accommodation.

During the pilgrimage, the pilgrims circulate not only on the two main unpaved village streets but also make several visits to Nan Palm, Saint Jean and Le Saut, all located less than half a mile from the village. Pilgrims go to those places because the Holy Virgin is supposed to have appeared at each one – and Damballah and Aidda Oueddo, two Voodoo spirits, are believed to live there permanently.

The Catholic church and the Voodoo temples are the two major religious institutions in the village. Protestants in Saut D'Eau number about 175, including Baptists and Seventh Day Adventists, and are mainly found in rural areas adjacent to Saut D'Eau. The major Protestant denomination, the Baptist church, is of recent origin in the village. It was introduced there by an American Baptist missionary minister, Lee Karoll, in 1948, almost a century after the apparitions of the Holy Virigin in Saut D'Eau.

THE DEVELOPMENT OF SAUT D'EAU AS A PILGRIMAGE CENTRE

The development of Saut D'Eau as a pilgrimage centre – that is, as an alternative shrine – was a reaction against the satellite or periphery status and the dependency character of Haitian pilgrims *vis-à-vis* the Nuestra Señora del Altagracia shrine in the Dominican Republic, where Haitians once flocked annually. The history of the village is linked with the history of its shrine, which attracts thousands of pilgrims from all over the country every year. Before the earthquake of 7 May 1842, which devastated Cap-Haitien – the second largest city in Haiti – and caused the formation of a majestic waterfall in Saut D'Eau, Saut D'Eau was simply a small district of the rural section of the Canot River (Rouzier 1891: 262).

It was only during the reign of Faustin Soulouque, president and then emperor of Haiti (1847–1859), that Saut D'Eau began to become a place of pilgrimage. The political as well as the economic situation of Haiti was deteriorating when Soulouque took office: Jean-Pierre Boyer, a former president for life (1818–1843), had succeeded in politically unifying the island – both Haiti and the Dominican Republic – during his regime, but after Boyer's fall, *'présidents de doublure'* (puppet presidents) were elected who spent only a few months in office. They were chosen by ambitious politicians and generals who took advantage of the office for promoting their own interests. In fact, Soulouque, a Voodoo practitioner, was named to serve his term as a puppet president, but he did not allow himself to be dominated by his political advisors.

In the early years of his reign, Soulouque faced three major political problems (Léger 1907: 197). First, he could not recapture easily the eastern portion of the island because the Dominican Republic, having been separated from Haiti in 1844, proclaimed its independence the same year. The new Republic had placed its army in a state of alert to prevent Haitian troops from invading once more its territory. The Haitians were suddenly cut off from their traditional pilgrimage centre of the island at Nuestra Señora de Altagracia del Higuey – Haitian pilgrims had been accustomed to crossing the border and journeying to this shrine every year. Second, the peasants of the south, namely the Piquets, revolted against their lack of land and their neglect by corrupt politicians. Third, Soulouque, uneducated and known for his repressive policies, had to crack down and find ways of solving problems raised by the presence of black and mulatto political factions in his government.

After the defeat of his military attempt to recover the Dominican portion of the island (6 March–6 May 1849), Soulouque decided to strengthen his authority at home. Searching for excuses to name himself emperor, Soulouque found an opportunity when a rumour that the Holy Virgin had appeared in a palm tree on the property of one Debarine in the Champ-de-Mars began circulating in Port-au-Prince (Cabon 1933: 45). Those who had seen the apparition declared that the Holy Virgin was covered with a mantle and a crown – and Soulouque interpreted the event as God's approbation for his coronation. This took place early in July, 1849.

Later, on 16 July of the same year, apparitions were reported in Saut D'Eau. Soulouque interpreted these events for the Haitian masses as a sign from God that he should become emperor.[2]

On Monday, 23 November 1849, with another rumour circulating that the Holy Virgin had again appeared in the Champ-de-Mars, the emperor's wife went to see the event. Her visit strengthened popular and national beliefs in the veracity of the apparitions.

The question of apparitions preoccupied Soulouque's government, and members of the legislative cabinet were appointed to study the phenomena of Saut D'Eau. Among the top officials appointed were Louis Dufresne (general of the army and minister of war, the navy and foreign relations), Jean-Baptiste Francisque (minister of justice, worship and public education) and Lysius Félicité Salomon (minister of finance). Upon receiving the report of this committee, Soulouque ordered that a chapel be built in Saut D'Eau in honour of the Holy Virgin. From then on, Saut D'Eau has become the national pilgrimage centre of the Republic of Haiti (Jolibois 1970b). The French missionary clergy were circumspect about the apparitions; Father Sapini, the pastor of Mirebalais who was in charge of conducting an inquiry on Saut D'Eau, showed some doubt about the authenticity of the apparitions (Jolibois 1970a). Other members of the missionary clergy, however, accepted the apparitions as genuine – Father Pisano for example, at that time pastor of Petionville, proclaimed the authenticity of the apparitions (Cabon 1933: 407).

When Saut D'Eau started to attract pilgrims, Faustin Soulouque changed the region's status from that of rural section of the River Canot to a military post (*poste militaire*). On 3 September 1885, President Lysius Félicité Salomon made Saut D'Eau a *quartier* and appointed a courtroom judge and a county officer to record births, marriages and deaths (Jolibois 1970c). Before this, the people of Saut D'Eau had depended on the county officer of Mirebalais. In 1904, on the order of President Nord Alexis (1902–1908), Saut D'Eau became a parish, and Julien Conan, then archbishop of Port-au-Prince, appointed a priest there on a permanent basis. On 28 January, 1911, President Antoine Simon (1908–1911) changed the status of Saut D'Eau again and made it a *commune*.[3]

Saudolese describe with emotion the miraculous apparitions of the Holy Virgin and remember from oral traditions the major dates in the history of the pilgrimage. The following narrative was collected from an 83-year-old Saudolese villager. This same story was recounted to me again and again by others, with some minor modifications.

During the regime of Faustin Soulouque, in 1849, a young man, Fortuné Morose, looked one morning for his horse which had left his garden the night before. In search of this animal, he penetrated a bush area not too far from the place where the village of Saut D'Eau is now located. Once he pushed his way in, a strange noise made by the rubbing of leaves attracted his attention. Great was his surprise to see a young lady inviting him to look at her. Despite the solicitations of this beautiful young lady, Morose was taken by fear and went to report the event to the nearest police station. A policeman was delegated to accompany Morose to be a witness to the event. Unhappily, the unknown lady did not show up when they arrived or they did not see her. A little bit later, they were still looking for her everywhere when the policeman turned his look toward a palm tree. Surprise. He saw a great and beautiful animated picture on a palm leaf. He invited Morose to look at the picture. Morose identified it as the picture of the lady that he had seen previously. Immediately they went out and announced the news to anyone that they could meet in the region.

From this time on, the people of the surrounding area came from time to time to see if the picture was still there and waited patiently until the leaf fell to observe it more closely. After about a month, the leaf fell and the picture was not on it. But the same picture was reproduced on another leaf. The news of the apparitions of the Holy Virgin in Saut D'Eau raced throughout the country. The place where the palm trees on which the Holy Virgin appeared is known as Nan Palm. It has become since then a holy place, and every 16 July, pilgrims make a trip to Saut D'Eau.

In the proximity of the well-known palm tree, a spring still flows. This source has miraculous power. For example, a young blind lady, Mme. Dorvilus Etiène, had heard about the apparitions. She asked somebody to drive her from Jacmel to Saut D'Eau. In Saut D'Eau, she washed her eyes with water taken from this spring, and after repeating this three days, she began to see again. To accomplish her vows to the Holy Virgin, she brought all of her children to Saut D'Eau, and every 16 July, her grandsons and granddaughters come in pilgrimage to Notre Dame du Mont Carmel shrine.

The Saudolese keep fresh in their memories the sad history of two priests who cut down the trees where the Holy Virgin had appeared. In 1891, under the administration of President Florvil Hyppolite, a French missionary named Father Lenouvel considered the tree of the first apparitions the locus for superstitious practices and cut it down. Having done so, he went to the church, lost consciousness, and died the same day – the faithful believe that he was thus punished for his sacrilegious act (Haïti Littéraire et Sociale, 1905). The pilgrims continued to venerate another palm tree in the vicinity of the original one. Driven by his missionary zeal to get rid of Voodooists in Saut D'Eau, another priest named Father Cessens cut down this second palm tree – strangely enough, this priest suffered a paralytic stroke and died a few months later. This occurrence strengthened the pilgrims' faith in the apparitions and was interpreted as the revenge of both the Holy Virgin and Voodoo spirits. The blessing of various Haitian governments of Saut D'Eau as the national pilgrimage centre and the faith of the Saudolese and the pilgrims have to some extent forced the Catholic clergy to accept this situation as a fact of life.

The miracles that seem to occur yearly in Saut D'Eau, the need to have a national shrine after the independence of the Dominican

Republic, the waterfall (the residence of Voodoo spirits) and the crowds that continue to come to Saut D'Eau every year are some of the elements accounting for the development of Saut D'Eau as the national pilgrimage centre.

THE PILGRIMS

Pilgrims start arriving one month before the day of the feast of Our Lady of Mount Carmel. They come from every corner of Haiti by foot, on horseback, and in trucks – very few arrive in private cars. A week before the feast, the *tap-taps* (small buses painted in loud colours) that normally travel between Carrefour and Port-au-Prince or Petionville and Port-au-Prince change their routes for Port-au-Prince to Saut D'Eau. On the morning of 16 July, chartered buses bring various groups of pilgrims to Saut D'Eau. Throughout the entire journey, pilgrims recite rosaries together and sing Christian songs to the Holy Virgin.

A large number of pilgrims come from the central plateau. They usually rent horses for eight days or so, bring their own luggage as well as feed for their animals, form groups of two, three, four, or five people and sing songs to encourage each other on the route to Saut D'Eau. These groups are organised on the basis of kinship, friendship and neighbourhood ties. When they arrive in Saut D'Eau, pilgrims stay together and may help each other financially if there is any need.

I have witnessed in Lascahobas, a village in the central plateau, how chartered buses are organised for the pilgrimage. At the beginning of July, a lady well known in the village told friends and neighbours that there would be a bus for Saut D'Eau and invited them to write their names on a list. When she had enough persons interested in the project, she went to make arrangements with a bus driver. On the day of the pilgrimage the bus was full (pilgrims did not have to pay for children who accompanied them). These village people all knew each other, and upon arriving in Saut D'Eau they decided where and when they would have to pick up the bus to go back home. They stayed together in groups of two or three and knew where the members of the other subgroups were in case of need.

In addition, also one month before the feast, mendicants and physically handicapped persons arrive in Saut D'Eau. Most of them come by foot, sometimes from the farthest corners of the island.

They come in the hope of a miracle, and in the belief that the Holy Virgin will better their lives. In this sense, they are also pilgrims – but they have other reasons for coming to Saut D'Eau. They know that they might obtain money and food from the wealthy Voodoo pilgrims who come there to distribute to the needy. These better-off pilgrims do so partly to fulfill vows to the Holy Virgin but, more important, to carry out the order of their local Voodoo priests.

At the front door of the Catholic church, in Saint Jean, Le Saut and Nan Palm, mendicants sit and wait in line, asking for charity in the name of God. They have a *coui* (plate) that they present to people who pass by. Upon receiving something, they bless the giver (*'moin mandé bon Dié poul béni ou'*) and thank the Holy Virgin for sending someone to them (*'mèsi manman la Vièg'*). One of the most common street scenes is that of pilgrims distributing food to the needy. For example, when coffee is being distributed, every mendicant stands around the giver and shows his *coui*. The giver must be careful to give something to everyone. Mendicant pilgrims sleep everywhere – on the doorsteps of the church, in the marketplace and on unoccupied porches.

Voodoo penitents circulate the streets of Saut D'Eau in every direction. They are people who are or have been sick, who have had bad luck or who simply believe that spirits are bothering them. Voodoo priests ask them to wear penitential clothes. Before their journey to Saut D'Eau, they are requested to attend Catholic mass every Sunday during the Lenten period and are invited to remain at the back of the church. Until their penance is over, they are not allowed to wash their penitential clothes. This custom was very popular before the anti-superstition campaign organised in the 1940s by French Catholic missionaries. Although Voodoo penitents still wear penitential clothes, they are allowed to wash them from time to time! Some women simply prefer to cover their *robe sac* with another clean dress. The *robe sac* is now disappearing more and more, even among peasants; instead, women wear blue or white clothing with white girdles around their waists and medals and scapulars around their necks.

The *'madan-sara'* (vendors) are everywhere in the village, selling everything from candles to clothes. They flood the Saut D'Eau public market with produce from Port-au-Prince or from surrounding villages. In front of the church, as well as in Nan Palm, Saint Jean, and Le Saut, they sell candles, medals, girdles, rosaries, chromolithographs of Catholic saints, candies and bread, as well as

Voodoo paraphernalia. In Saut D'Eau, the church keeps no shop where pilgrims may buy religious articles, and this function is taken on by *madan-sara*.

Prostitutes from Port-au-Prince and from other cities, as well as gamblers, arrive in Saut D'Eau one week before the feast. These prostitutes and the *madan-sara* consider themselves pilgrims and attend church services. The prostitutes come often to the church to ask the Holy Virgin a favour – that of sending them good clients. They pray that the Holy Virgin intercede so that they may gain financial profit from their trip to Saut D'Eau, and they make donations to the church and vow to donate even more if the Holy Virgin does send them clients! Their job, as they perceive it, does not serve as a barrier to good relations with the Holy Virgin; instead, it allows them to bargain with her.

Gamblers bring various kinds of gambling tables into Saut D'Eau. Their tactics are to allow peasants to win once, and after that to empty their pockets. During the day, gamblers gather around small gambling tables that are placed in proximity to the public market. At night, they assemble in the vicinity of the Catholic church, waiting for pilgrims who have attended the novena. Because there is no electricity in Saut D'Eau, they use *lampes-têtes-gridappes* (peasant lamps) at night.

A few days before the feast, nearby Catholic priests arrive to help the pastor of Saut D'Eau. During this period, more donations for masses are recorded than during the rest of the year altogether. Pilgrims who have received special favours from the Holy Virgin fill the pastor's office to pay for masses. Voodooists who have collected money for the Holy Virgin and Damballah from other peasants in their home villages bring it at this time to the priest in charge of the shrine.

In the streets, some pilgrims sing songs to the Holy Virgin while others may gather around someone who is possessed by a spirit. There is an air of gaiety in the village – the pilgrims have fulfilled their vows and feel renewed.

Pilgrims come to Saut D'Eau for many reasons: to make a promise or to accomplish a vow, to give thanks, to acquire good luck in order to make money, to follow the orders of Voodoo priests, to get married or to beget a child. For both Catholics and Voodooists, Saut D'Eau is a spiritual centre, a place to renew good relationships with the supernatural world.

The pilgrims pass through sequential phases that can be seen in terms of rites of passage (Van Gennep 1960). In this process, there are ways of identifying instances of separation (with the departure from home to start the journey), instances of transition (the journey is a kind of rebirth, a rite of purification; the pilgrims are aware that the journey is not a permanent venture and that they must go back home after the feast or after they have paid a visit to the shrine), and finally re-incorporation (the rite of returning to their familial milieu and their original community).

Pilgrims make their journeys to a shrine in order to reduce structural distances between themselves and a spiritual centre, a centre of energy. The journey represents for them a symbolic passage from periphery to centre – one marches them from a satellite position to a specific centre. Pilgrimage is thus the process of separating oneself from a peripheral situation to move – not permanently – to a centre position in order to reaffirm and strengthen one's faith. In the Muslim tradition the Koran prescribes that one should make a pilgrimage at least once in one's life, but in the Christian tradition, pilgrimage is an act of free piety (Fahd 1973: 68). Pilgrimage is a process of affirmation of faith through a symbolic death for a spiritual rejuvenation.

FOLK CHRISTIANITY AND VOODOO PRACTICES

Before the pilgrimage begins, relatives and friends remaining at home ask the pilgrims to pray for them and to bring back medals of the Holy Virgin. It is not important for everyone to go there, but someone in the family should make the trip. As soon as they arrive in Saut D'Eau, pilgrims buy medals and scapulars and ask a priest to bless them. They then wear some of them and take the others home to their children and relatives.

The pilgrims' religion is one of vows and promises (Marzal 1967; Gross 1971; Turner 1974; Laguerre 1969) – they come to Saut D'Eau to make or accomplish a vow. This interchange with the Holy Virgin is strict – she gives something, but it is important to fulfil the vow in order to avoid falling ill or having bad luck. The harmony will not be broken if one does what one has promised to do.

Nine days before the feast, there is a novena in honour of the Holy Virgin. This is an evening worship from 7 to 10 pm and interspersed with the recitation of the rosary are songs to the Holy Mary. The church is crowded, and one must be there by about 6 pm to secure a seat – in the aisles, as well as outside the church, those without seats remain standing. During the entire week the pastor comments on the role of Mary in the church and the history of the Holy Virgin's apparitions throughout the world. Candles burn throughout the service and during the collection pilgrims offer money or candles. Each night toward the end of the service, the pastor admonishes the pilgrims not to attend Voodoo services or to organise and participate in public dances; instead, he invites the assembly to meditate and to pray.

On the day of the feast, the crowd assembled in the church for the procession through the village. Altar boys with a cross lead the procession, followed by the children in two lines, the women, the priests in front of the float on the top of which the statue of the Holy Virgin stands and finally the group of men. The float is elaborately decorated with flowers and oriflammes, and the procession passes through the main streets of the village while the pilgrims recite rosaries and, at intervals, sing.

Most of the houses on the main streets are decorated with plants and flowers. Mass is celebrated and an invited priest delivers the homily. In the church, the statue of the Holy Virgin attracts the attention of the pilgrims, who pray with their hands open during the consecration, imploring the mercy of God. After mass, everyone wants to kiss or at least to touch the statue.

A crucifixion scene, placed at the entry to the village, also attracts pilgrims who light candles and talk aloud to the 'suffering' Christ. Staying on their knees, they open their arms while they gaze fixedly at the crucifix – they also touch and kiss the base of the crucifix three times. Before leaving, they put candles and flowers on the altar of the calvary, and at the front door of the calvary, as well as in front of the church, pilgrims burn candles – not for the Holy Virgin, but for the *loa* (spirit) Legba, guardian of all entrances.

Other elements of folk Christianity can also be perceived among prostitutes and Voodooists in their dealings with the church. According to the church, extramarital sexual relations are sinful. The prostitutes themselves do not see anything wrong in prostituting themselves to better their lives economically, they see prostitution rather as a survival strategy and they ask the Holy Virgin to intercede for them. Although they feel rejected by the church, they still believe in belonging to some kind of spiritual or Christian community. They also believe that what the community of men cannot understand, the Holy Virgin does. Someone who is not aware of the situation may find it strange that the same ladies who were in the brothels the night before come to participate in the church services early in the morning. Voodooist prostitutes make several visits to Le Saut and wash themselves in the water where Damballah and Aidda Oueddo are believed to live.

About one month before the feast, Voodooists collect money from door to door in their own villages to offer to the Holy Virgin. People who will not be able to go to Saut D'Eau give some money in the belief that these Voodooists will bring it to Our Lady of Mount Carmel. In the streets of Saut D'Eau these same Voodooists again go from door to door asking for money for the Holy Virgin. If someone asks them why they are making this collection, they give the name of the *loas* (spirits) who have asked for this kind of penance – the money is then given to Saut D'Eau's pastor to say a solemn mass for them. This is a penitential act, and a Voodoo priest may ask any penitent to perform it in order to restore good relations with the *loa* that has been offended.

Voodoo pilgrims gather in Le Saut, Nan Palm and Saint Jean because these places are loci of previous apparitions of the Holy Virgin, but followers of two aquatic Voodoo spirits called Damballah and Aidda Oueddo also make the journey to Saut D'Eau to venerate them. In Le Saut, people toss money into the water, light candles, bathe for good luck, become possessed and make predictions. In the proximity of the spirits, pilgrims feel themselves to be in another world.

In Saint Jean, Nan Palm, and Le Saut, pilgrims not only wash themselves in the spring, but they also hang ribbons around trees, believing that most of the trees in this area are inhabited by spirits.[4] Before leaving, they take some water with them to be poured into the basins of Voodoo temples sacred to Damballah and Aidda Oueddo.

Nan Palm is the place where the Virgin Mary first appeared, according to the oral tradition started by the Saudolese. The original tree has been cut down, but pilgrims still believe that *loas* inhabit the neighbouring trees. These trees are choked with votive girdles. Soil taken from the base of the palm trees is mixed with other ingredients and used as an unguent in Voodoo temples. Lighted candles, girdles, food, and money are presented to Damballah and Aidda, while pilgrims repeat prayers that *mambo* (Voodoo priestesses) and *houngan* (Voodoo priests) recite, and *houngans* talk to the *loas* and ask them special favours for sick Voodooists.

Voodoo pilgrims do not go alone to Nan Palm, Le Saut, and Saint Jean – they are accompanied by relatives, friends, or quite often by Voodoo priests and *mambo*. This is a technical precaution to avoid being drowned, for by the time they become possessed someone needs to take care of them. Other people gather round them while they are possessed to salute the *loas* and to listen to their predictions. Voodoo and bush priests officiate as folk physicians in Nan Palm, Le Saut and Saint Jean. The penitents who accompany them distribute food to the mendicants in response to the demand of *loas* protectors – on their knees, they pray to the *loas* who inhabit the trees and kiss the soil three times before leaving.

In the streets of Saut D'Eau, Voodooists become possessed and are surrounded by other pilgrims. They speak for their *loa* protectors and make predictions in a jargon that is difficult to understand. Their eyes are wide open, their limbs are well stretched and they are out of themselves – possessed. Scenes of this kind provoke spontaneous gatherings from time to time in the streets of Saut D'Eau.

In Le Saut, Nan Palm and Saint Jean, I witnessed Voodoo priests sitting under trees with large containers of Voodoo concoction in front of them. They used it for curing and healing purposes when a Voodoo devotee came to them. Passing Voodoo priests came to shake hands with them and to find out which degree they had reached in the Voodoo hierarchy – instances of spirit possession were also observed in these circumstances. In the evenings, more devotees gathered round the priests and they participated in Voodoo dances.

Saut D'Eau is a Christian as well as a Voodoo centre. The distinction between folk Christianity and Voodoo practices is not made by Voodooists because one needs to be a Christian in order to belong to a Voodoo congregation – there is such a mixture in the pilgrims' religious practices that it is difficult to see where folk Christianity ends and Voodoo starts. Voodoo priests commonly order devotees to make a pilgrimage to Saut D'Eau during their initiation to the *hounsi canzo* degree (first degree in the Voodoo hierarchy) and before their ordination to the Voodoo priesthood. In this sense, one can understand why some mendicants are accomplishing a religious obligation when they beg for money that they later give to the Catholic priest in Saut D'Eau. Saut D'Eau is the only place during the feast of Our Lady of Mount Carmel where one can find in the same niche all the varieties of Voodoo tradition on the island. By coming to Saut D'Eau, Voodoo priests try to attract national attention and to gain national recognition for the Voodoo church, which has a peripheral status in contrast to the Catholic church – the state church – which has a central status.

USE OF THE HOLY VIRGIN'S APPARITIONS IN HAITIAN POLITICS

The first apparitions were interpreted by Faustin Soulouque as a national event. Initially, he made people believe that the apparitions were a sign of God's approbation for his accession to the throne as emperor of Haiti,[5] but eventually, by recognising the authenticity of the apparitions of Saut D'Eau, he encouraged soldiers as well as peasants to believe that the Holy Virgin was with him and on the side of the Haitian army in their efforts to recapture the Dominican Republic (Aubin 1910: 93).

During the occupation of Haiti by US marines (1915–1934), Haitian guerrillas used the name of the Holy Virgin of Saut D'Eau to incite peasants to struggle against them. These political guerrilla leaders interpreted US presence in their country as being against the will of the Holy Virgin and the heroes of the struggle for independence. Thus, peasant resistance to liberate the country was animated by their patriotic feeling and sustained by this religious ideology.

Wearing around their necks the Holy Virgin scapulars and medals blessed in Saut D'Eau, many peasants engaged in guerrilla warfare in the mountains of Pensez-y-Bien, Crochus and Morne-à-Cabrit and strengthened their solidarity with other bands under the leadership of Charlemagne Péralte and Benoît Batraville, who struggled in the regions of Lascahobas, Belladère and Mirebalais. Despite their lack of weapons – trusting only in the scapulars they wore – they were able to attack successfully the US military station in Croix-des-Bouquets, and with the help of General Codio by May 1916 they had occupied Croix-des-Bouquets. Against these peasants, the US placed 800 soldiers on the *Habitation Leroux*, 400 in Montet, three kilometres north of Carrefour-de-Beaurepos and another regiment in Terre-Rouge (Jolibois, 1970d).

The US was aware of the political use made of the apparitions by the guerrillas – this was one of the reasons why a marine posted in Mirebalais ordered one of the palm trees of Saut D'Eau cut down, for this palm tree was an object of veneration to the peasants. A few days later the marine became sick and was sent back to the US, thus reinforcing the peasant belief that the Holy Virgin was against the US occupation of Haiti.

Haitian politicians are aware of how the apparitions have been used against foreign enemies, although no movement has yet been initiated from Saut D'Eau by any group of pilgrims or others using the Holy Virgin's name to incite the masses to overthrow any Haitian government. Nevertheless, the possibility seems to be latent. This was clearly understood when the Haitian government prohibited students from taking part in the pilgrimage of 1964. It was believed that the political situation was at such a climax that any movement initiated under the Holy Virgin's name could overthrow the Haitian government.

Since the reign of Soulouque, the Haitian government has had *manu militari* as well as symbolic control over the national pilgrimage centre. During the period of the feast, detectives and policemen are sent there so that the government may have absolute control over the situation. Every year the president sends his financial contribution to Saut D'Eau's pastor, who in turn announces it to the congregation – like any other pilgrim, the president in this way fulfills his vows. He is believed to be a pilgrim even without coming to Saut D'Eau, and because of his financial contribution to the Holy Virgin many pilgrims feel sympathetic toward him.

PILGRIMAGE AND THE MAINTENANCE OF SOCIAL ORDER

This pilgrimage is in various ways functional to the system. It plays an integrative role at village level by opening channels of communications among villagers. Groups of villagers make the trip together and get to know and are bound up with one another – making new friends is a positive element as far as village cohesiveness and unity are concerned. The case of Voodooists who pass from door to door to collect money for the Holy Virgin is a good example of how social integration occurs at village level. One collects the money this year; someone else will do so next year. This simple act reinforces solidarity and friendship among people of the same village.

For the Saudolese the pilgrimage generates a periodic cash flow. Besides being able to sell their products at good prices (some store rice, beans and corn, waiting for the coming of pilgrims to sell them), they also make a little money by renting rooms in their homes. The pilgrimage relieves the monotony of village life as the Saudolese participate in the 'pilgrimage cycle'. They live and adapt themselves to the 'in-between pilgrimage' situation, but after the feast is over, the Saudolese look forward to the next one – this gives them a sense of hope.

For the mendicants, the pilgrimage plays the role of a non-existent Haitian welfare bureau. For at least a month, the mendicant is provided with food and some money. The trip to Saut D'Eau also has a mininal effect on the distribution of the population of Haiti. After the feast of Our Lady of Saut D'Eau, a few of the mendicants move to Port-au-Prince, thereby increasing the population of the slum areas of the capital.

Supposedly, the pilgrimage – by bringing people from different class statuses together – should help break down class barriers among the pilgrims. However, class barriers remain. Mulattoes do not mingle with peasants, and in fact, the mulattoes and educated blacks look down upon the peasant Voodooists. Equally, those who come with their private cars, speak French and are well mannered can be distinguished from the crowd of peasants. The pilgrimage therefore provides a microscopic view of class structure in Haitian society.

Pilgrims of the same village manifest solidarity amongst themselves and also toward others, but they experience the feeling of brotherhood more deeply with people of their own groups and with friends. They may refrain from becoming involved with other people because of the fear and rivalry that exists among Voodooists. Thus, the pilgrims experience a certain communal harmony in their respective subgroups, but also, more or less, a *cassure* or disharmony with the community of pilgrims taken as a whole.

Peasant pilgrims do not come to Saut D'Eau for practical political purposes, they come to accomplish private vows, to visit the shrine and to communicate their problems to the Holy Virgin. They come for personal reasons, hoping that their situation will change for the better in the near future. Even when a trip to the shrine is organised for a group, each individual has his own projects and vows – there are definitely no common projects. It is not that the villagers nourish a cult of fatalism and resignation; rather, they look for individual alleviation. They are more motivated to change their spiritual and economic situation than to struggle for change at either a local or national level.

The pilgrimage promotes the development of continuous religious syncretism among the peasants less in terms of 'material acculturation'

(Bastide 1970: 144) than in terms of *weltanschauung*. Voodoo *loas* and Catholic saints are in proximity to each other. By invoking the Holy Virgin and/or Damballah Oueddo, pilgrims strengthen their ties with the supernatural world and gain enough spiritual force to live by until the next pilgrimage. The pilgrims leave their problems in the hands of the Holy Virgin and/or Damballah and hope that these sources of spiritual help will solve their problems at their earliest convenience.

CONCLUSION

Although there are several pilgrimage centres in Haiti, Saut D'Eau remains the main one and stands as a national symbol for the whole country. In the past, Haitian politicians have used the apparitions of the Holy Virgin in Saut D'Eau to make peasants fight against Dominican guerrillas and against US marines – however, the apparitions have not historically been exploited to overthrow any Haitian regime.

The pilgrimage makes it possible for pilgrims to renew good relations both with the Holy Virgin and the Voodoo *loas*. In Saut D'Eau, *loas* and saints maintain good relations and are symbolic of the harmony – so the Voodoo peasants believe – that must exist among Haitians. The pilgrims feel fulfilled by accomplishing their vows or *promesa*. All the pilgrims – the penitents, the voodooists, the mendicants, the *madan-sara*, the prostitutes, and the gamblers – gain spiritually, psychologically or economically by going to Saut D'Eau.

The fact that pilgrims come to Saut D'Eau in search of individual alleviation, with the consequent lack of a common political project; their belief in the Holy Virgin and/or Voodoo spirits as solely capable of solving their problems; the effect of the pilgrimage on the social cohesiveness of other villages; the harmonious marriage between folk Christianity and Voodoo in Saut D'Eau, and government control to avoid having the Voodoo priests in their trance make predictions against the elected president of the Republic. These are the variables which explain why apart from any period of crisis during which the Haitian regime faces foreign enemies, the pilgrimage is functional to the maintenance of the social system.

7 Politics and Voodoo During the Duvalier Era

One of the most intriguing aspects of Haitian governmental politics during the Duvalier era was its pervasive ramifications and far-reaching influence on the Voodoo belief system and its co-optation of local Voodoo leaders (Manigat 1964). It is not possible to fully understand the functioning of local Haitian politics over the past two decades without paying attention to the pivotal role played by some Tontons Macoutes (militiamen), who were also influential Voodoo priests in their communities (Diederich and Burt 1969; Laguerre 1982a). During the administrations of François 'Papa Doc' [1957–71] and Jean-Claude 'Baby Doc' [1971–86] Duvalier, Voodoo became so central in the organisation of the Haitian political system that its political content deserves further analysis.[1]

The politicisation of Voodoo was first discussed by Jean Price-Mars (1928), who linked the success of the Haitian Revolution to the commanding role played by Voodooist insurrectionist leaders. Jean Price-Mars went as far as to say that, had it not been for Voodooist participation in the revolutionary movement, Haiti would not have become an independent nation in 1804. François Duvalier and Lorimer Denis in their celebrated essay, '*L'Evolution Stadiale du Vodou*,' published in 1944, reached a similar conclusion. They also suggested that the events of the Haitian Revolution have had a tremendous influence on Voodoo ethno-theology in that a few of the heroic leaders were thereafter canonised Voodoo spirits (Duvalier 1968a: 178). One had to wait until 1958 to see a full historical documentation and analysis of Voodoo during the wars of independence (Mennesson-Rigaud 1958).

The use of Voodoo by the Duvalier regime has been the subject of several studies. For example, Manigat (1964) has suggested that Papa Doc had a few Voodoo priests who served as his special assistants, and that with their help he was able to reach and control a section of Haitian society. Montilus (1972) notes that in contrast to the repressive measures against Voodoo taken by previous administrations, the Duvalier regime was most sympathetic to Voodooists. The historical evolution of the interplay between Voodoo and politics was taken up by Rotberg (1976), who saw Papa Doc as the Voodoo priest *par excellence* who used Voodoo to mystify the masses. David Nicholls's (1970) analysis of religion and politics in Haiti touches only tangentially on Voodoo and more substantially on the Catholic and Episcopal churches. On a more speculative level, Hurbon (1979a) discusses Papa Doc's manipulation of the negritude and Voodoo ideology in order to legitimise his power over the masses. In a more recent study of local level politics in an urban slum in downtown Port-au-Prince, the participation of the Voodoo priests in the affairs of the state and their community was brought into light and substantiated (Laguerre 1982a).

It was the late Rémy Bastien (1966) who painstakingly analysed the relationship between Duvalierist politics and the Voodoo church. Living in exile, he was unable to substantiate some of his pronouncements, but he was the first to pinpoint the need to analyse 'the relationship between Duvalier and *vodoun* . . . from the standpoint of the relations between church and state' (Bastien 1966: 56). This implies a recognition of the state and Voodoo as two separate and distinct entities and furthermore suggests that the Voodoo church maintains its own autonomy *vis-à-vis* the rest of society.

I propose to look at Voodoo and politics as two poles of the same continuum. This approach reflects my way of dissecting Haitian national culture as comprising, on the one hand, the dominant Western-oriented culture and, on the other, the mass-based popular culture, both of them meshed together as each integrates selected elements from the other. The relationship between elite culture and popular culture must be seen as an expression of asymmetrical relationships between the dominant sector of society and the exploited masses.

To understand the interplay between Duvalierist politics and Voodoo, one must bear in mind that François Duvalier integrated into his regime the political aspect of Voodoo, the one that accounts for the independence of the island according to Duvalier's own interpretation and that perpetuates the mark of African civilisation on the matrix of Haitian society and culture.[2] Thus, it is less the Voodoo ritual that was retained than the political significance of the Voodoo church and the structure of relationships that it generates. The two Duvalier administrations appropriated the political aspect of Voodoo and consequently made the church an ideological symbol, part of the national political culture.

The root of the use of Voodoo in Duvalierist politics must be sought in François Duvalier's own writings before he even entered the field of politics.[3] One is forced to turn the clock back to the period between the two World Wars. Duvalier and his collaborator, Lorimer Denis – both of them disciples of Price-Mars – set for themselves the task of validating the culture of the masses as a reaction to the humiliation of the US occupation (1915–1934) and the cultural '*bovarysme*' (ambivalence) of the pro-Western mulatto elite.

FRANÇOIS DUVALIER AND THE GRIOTS GROUP

In any dependency context, the elite play the role of brokers linking the centre to the periphery. Although they are more often political and economic middlemen, they also play an ideological role because any system of domination, subjugation and exploitation tends to develop its own ideological apparatus to justify itself (Santos 1968). With their nationalist philosophy and criticisms of the ideological practices of the traditional bourgeoisie, the members of the Griots group – among them François Duvalier – aspired to become the new brokers of the nation. They purported to accomplish their goal by taking into account local customs and ways of life.

François Duvalier was one of the founders of the journal *Les Griots*, which, on 23 June 1938, published its declaration of intent. According to the editorial, the journal was to serve as a vehicle 'to formulate the literary and scientific doctrine' of the Griots group (Duvalier 1968a: 35). The October–December 1938 issue presented the essential points of the group's philosophy. They wrote that 'all our effort from independence to this day has consisted of a systematic repression of our African heritage . . . Our goal now is to recognise and accept our racial background' (Duvalier 1968a: 38).

With the goal of validating the folk culture of the masses, Duvalier began to study Voodoo with the intent of showing not only its African roots, but also its influence on national politics during the period of the wars of independence (Denis and Duvalier 1944). He came to the conclusion that a religion that served as a catalyst for national unity and that was part of Haiti's folk culture should not be denigrated, but maintained.[4] It did not take him long to realise that the people loved their Voodoo and it was the elite who despised it (Denis and Duvalier 1955).

At the time Duvalier formulated his Voodoo heritage statement, the Catholic church fervently opposed the practice of Voodoo in rural and urban Haiti.[5] The general policy of the Catholic church was to campaign against superstition (Roumain 1937). The campaign, which went on until the late 1950s, forced Voodooists to present their cultic objects and paraphernalia to their parish priest to be burned. It also forced them to take an oath of loyalty to the Catholic church, swearing that they would miraculously die if they ever practised Voodoo again.

The battle of some middle-class intellectuals – including François Duvalier – against church practice was opposed in Port-au-Prince by, among others, the priests of the Catholic newspaper *La Phalange*. One proponent of the anti-Voodoo policy of the Catholic church, Father Joseph Foisset, became the focus of attention of these young writers, among them François Duvalier and Lorimer Denis (Duvalier 1968a: 403–408). The latent animosity between Duvalier and the French clergy developed during those years.

For Duvalier, Voodoo had to be preserved at all costs because it represented the authentic soul of the Haitian people (Duvalier 1968a: 277–285). The rehabilitation of Voodoo meant that the struggle would have to be fought against the ideology of the pro-Western elite and the European clergy who had tried to dismiss things African and co-opt the Haitian people into Western civilisation. No doubt, to be successful, such a battle needed to be fought in the political arena. And the various studies that Duvalier wrote or co-authored had only one goal: to show that the Voodooists were the authentic Haitians, making up the majority of the population, and that they had fought for the independence of the republic and had been kept in poverty and out of mainstream politics. It was time to bring them into the mainstream of Haitian politics and to liberate them from their position of subordination *vis-à-vis* the French Catholic church and the pro-Western mulatto elite (Duvalier 1967). We will see that once Duvalier became president, he delivered a fatal blow to these two groups. At the same time, he nominated certain influential Voodoo priests to serve as his advisors and permitted Voodoo people to practise their religion openly with state protection.

VOODOO AND ELECTORAL POLITICS

The success of national brokers in maintaining their position depends a great deal on the support they received from local brokers. Electoral politics provides a situational context for understanding these structural links of dependency between both centre and periphery. This is one facet of the articulation of imperialism at national and local levels.

Before the Duvalier era, during the electoral campaigns, one could especially observe how the politicians manipulated Voodoo people in order to enhance their own popularity. Bastien (1966: 56) wrote, 'candidates to an elective office . . . cultivate the friendship of the key *houngans* [Voodoo priests] of their district, make donations to their temples, offer ceremonies and in addition, go to mass every Sunday.' He adds that they depend on 'the support and the favourable influence the *houngan* will exercise upon the electorate' (Bastien 1966: 56). Manigat (1964: 29) has made a similar observation: 'as for the *houngans*, they are frequently flattered by politicians, eager to use for their own career and influence the moral authority these Voodoo priests exert upon the masses . . . the politicians know how to form their own circles of *houngans* in order to control the local population and insure popularity.'

In the late 1940s, the Haitian Parliament passed a bill making it obligatory for the president to be elected by popular vote and not solely by the senators and the chamber of representatives (Weil *et al.* 1973: 109). During the elections of 1950, presidential and legislative candidates began to flirt more openly with influential Voodoo priests (and Catholic priests as well) to enlist their collaboration and their votes and the support of their followers. It was probably with the elections of 1957 that the ability of Voodoo priests to deliver votes was taken more seriously and was also proven to be effective (Laguerre 1982a: 97–126).

During the presidential campaign in 1957, François Duvalier enlisted the aid of a number of Voodoo priests. They were mostly men from Port-au-Prince who had served as informants when he wrote his analyses of Haitian Voodoo (Laguerre 1982a; Duvalier 1968a). Some of them – quite influential in the slums of Port-au-Prince – were familiar faces at the Institute of Ethnology. Through these priests and supporters, Duvalier was also able to enlist the help of other priests in the countryside (Laguerre 1982a). One of the strategies of the Duvalier campaign at the local level was to formally request the help of these politically conscious Voodoo priests. In fact, some of them used their temples as local headquarters of the Duvalier campaign.

The sympathy that Duvalier displayed toward the Voodooists made him less acceptable to the Catholic clergy and consequently unsuitable, in the minds of the elite, for the highest office in the land.

The fact that Catholic clergy were preaching during the electoral campaign to vote Catholic and not Voodoo not only turned the pro-indigenist native clergy pro-Duvalier, but also strengthened the Catholic vote for the light-skinned mulatto presidential candidate Louis Déjoie.

Voodooists were easily able to distinguish their candidate from that of the Catholic clergy, however. The equation Duvalier = Voodoo was established by the Catholic church itself; Duvalier did not present himself as a Voodoo candidate. In fact, he even complained about it. He wrote in a speech delivered in Port-de-Paix on 19 March 1957, that 'because my humble contribution to the study of some social phenomena deals with aspects of Haitian folklore, some people less informed in the domain of cultural anthropology have attempted to establish an insidious confusion between these phenomena which have been the subject of my studies and my religious convictions' (Duvalier 1968b: 172).

Duvalier also complained more generally about the negative image that the French clergy were projecting of him. He later spoke of 'the campaign of denigration' that Jean Robert, Bishop of Gonaives, had organised against him during the course of the presidential campaign (Duvalier 1968b: 90). At the peak of the electoral campaign he went to present his political platform to the editorial staff of the Catholic newspaper *La Phalange*, and afterwards complained that 'they preferred to present in an unfavourable way the future President of Haiti' (Duvalier 1968b: 140).

One must remember that throughout the electoral campaign the Catholic church's anti-superstition crusade was still going strong. It was evidently to most Voodooists' advantage to vote for François Duvalier as a way of protecting their church. After the two other black presidential candidates – Daniel Fignolé in exile in New York and Clément Jumelle – had withdrawn from the race, Duvalier became the natural leader of the masses. The Voodooists' sympathy toward the presidential candidate strongly benefited him at the polls and contributed in no insignificant way to his victory. That Voodoo priests could muster a significant number of votes on behalf of a presidential candidate became an unquestionable political reality during the elections of 1957.

THE VOODOOISATION OF HAITIAN POLITICS

From the standpoint of national politics, the dependency process conveys the idea of two poles involved in an asymmetrical type of relationship. In such a structure, the national brokers exert their political domination over the masses through the complicity of local leaders who serve as peripheral brokers. Starting in 1957, the Voodooisation of Haitian politics became a means to control the local institutions of the masses and to maintain that structure of inequality. We will see later exactly how the Duvalier administration was able to exploit local centres of power such as the Voodoo church.

After Duvalier had been elected president, the Catholic church, and especially its Breton clergy, headed on a collision course with his administration. The end result was that several priests were expelled or removed from their lucrative posts in Port-au-Prince (Pierre-Charles 1973: 76–78).

Here we have described a battle of ideologies in which François Duvalier was a participant. He identified himself with the masses and promoted their dreams and religious aspirations in reaction against a dominant ideology. More precisely, Duvalier's support of Voodoo became a battle for the control of the national religious space which was totally dominated by the Catholic church and its ideological apparatus. The marginal religious space used by the Voodoo church was fragile because it did not have any legal status. It survived only at the mercy of those who held political office at national and local levels. The presidency of François Duvalier had the curative effect of giving some form of legitimacy to the Voodoo church (Rotberg 1976). The politicisation of Voodoo was made possible because of the open support it gained from the administrations of François and Jean-Claude Duvalier.

Among all the twentieth century presidents of Haiti or Haitian administrations, the Duvaliers were the only ones who openly supported Voodooists in their attempt at national recognition. One of the innovative moves of François Duvalier's administration was to bring Voodoo into the open in the political process by co-opting Voodoo priests as brokers and Tontons Macoutes in their respective communities and by openly sponsoring Voodoo liturgies on behalf of his government (Diederich and Burt 1969).

I see the Voodooisation of Haitian politics in two distinct ways: in the use of Voodoo by national political leaders and in the participation of Voodoo priests in national and local level politics. The fact that politicians have sometimes been Voodoo believers is not a new phenomenon – what is new is public recognition of it. Some influential people in the Duvalier administrations have been known to be Voodooists – they were chosen not only because of their support for Duvalier during the electoral campaign, but also because they enabled him to tip the balance of power in certain regions. For example, in *the Département* of Artibonite, the most important authority was a Voodoo priest Tonton Macoute. His position as special representative of the president in the region was created as a way of neutralising the power of the local bishop, who happened to be one of the staunchest anti-Voodooists and anti-Duvalierists of the Catholic clergy (Duvalier 1969). Later the dismissal of the bishop and the nomination of one of his native priests to head the Ministry of Education was part of the general trend of the 'Duvalierisation' of both the Catholic and Voodoo churches.

One cabinet minister during the Papa Doc administration saw fit to build his own Voodoo temple in the Carrefour area. Evidently, he was not the only top-ranking government official involved (Diederich and Burt 1969). Throughout the country there were also individual Voodoo practitioners who held key government positions, but the Voodoo apparatus of the government became known through the participation of the palace personnel in Voodoo ceremonies on the eve of the celebrations of 22nd May, the day of national renewal (Laguerre 1982a). It was known that, on the eve of these celebrations, advisors to the president and other government officials came to the countryside to participate in Voodoo thanksgiving ceremonies on behalf of the permanent regime. The point I am making here is not that François Duvalier believed or paid for these ceremonies, but that they seem to have received his blessings – at least, he did not care to stop them.

One of Papa Doc's boldest moves was to have incorporated Voodoo priests in his government, especially at the local level. Voodoo priests served as informants, spying on members of their congregation, and as Tontons Macoutes within the boundaries of their communities and neighbourhoods (Laguerre 1982a). Through the network of Voodoo priests, it was possible to reach the masses and also to control them. Their temples were used for the diffusion of the Duvalierist ideology.

Several writers have stated erroneously that Voodoo temples are isolated from each other and that a clever politician needs to deal with them on a one-to-one basis (Bastien 1966; Métraux 1958). This is evidently not true and is the result of a misunderstanding of the structure of relationships generated by the Voodoo churches.

The majority of Voodoo churches are part of a network controlled by a single temple that functions as the primary node of that network. Satellite or associate temples that are attached to the node belong either to the priest, his common-law wife or individuals who have obtained their training through the central temple. They continue to maintain their kinship and ritual ties to the primal core.

In one of the Upper Belair temples that I studied, the priest owned two temples: one in Port-au-Prince and the other in Cayes. The Port-au-Prince temple was connected to two other satellite temples one in Carrefour and the other in Cité St Martin (each is a district in the Port-au-Prince metropolitan area). In Cayes, his temple was connected to a satellite temple in the periphery of the city and to another one in a southern village.

These connections were made possible because the priests in the satellite temples had been trained through the owner of the central temple in Port-au-Prince and Cayes. They remained loyal to him, maintained contact with his temples and sometimes sent complicated cases of illness to him for cure. In addition, they all belonged to the same secret society.

A network of Voodoo churches can be established for several different reasons. For example, the priests of satellite temples may train through the central church – in such a situation, the relationship between the central church and the peripheral temples ends up being asymmetrical. One can also think of a network of churches based on consanguineal relationships. In Upper Belair, for example, a Voodoo priest married a woman from Croix-des-Bouquets whose father had a temple there. Over the years, there was a blending of Voodoo traditions in both temples – although each kept its own autonomy. These temples developed a *modus vivendi* that allowed them to collaborate and complement each other.

The following diagrams show the distribution or network of Voodoo temples in relation to a central unit.

In a universe of n temples ($A_1 \ldots A_n$), each temple can influence only its own members. if, as illustrated in Model I, $n=9$, then one has nine independent temples with no interconnection. Anyone wanting to influence the voting patterns of all the temples must contact each one separately. In this case, $x(\text{contacts})=9$.

The first model presents a situation where each temple is autonomous but may be part of a *lakou* (extended family compound) arrangement. By and large Voodoo temples that are isolated and

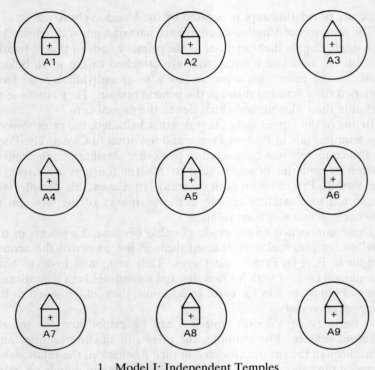

1   Model I: Independent Temples

autonomous units are geared toward domestic cults and do not attract the general public.

In Model II, there are three independent temples (A2, A3, and A9) and three sets of temples with symmetrical relationships (A1A4, A5A6, and A7A8). Anyone wanting to influence the nine temples need only contact each one of the three independent temples and one in each set of temples; $x=6$.

The second model presents a case where two temples previously separated and isolated from each other have become connected through the marriage of one of the priests to someone in the other temple. No temple here is in any position of structural superiority in relation to the other. In fact, their link is maintained through a restrained symmetrical relationship.

In Model III, there are three independent temples (A3, A7, and A9) and two sets of temples (A1A2, A1A4, A4A2 and A5A6, A5A8,

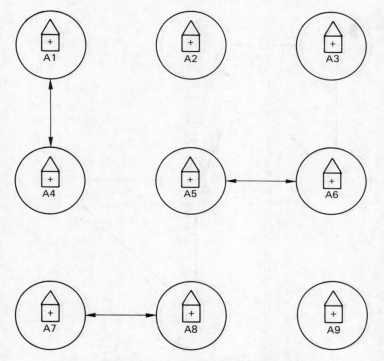

2   Model II: Temples with Symmetrical Relationships

A8A6), each temple in a set headed by the same Voodoo priest. To influence all the congregations in this universe, one needs to contact the three independent temples and one temple in each of the two sets; $x=5$.

The third model presents a situation where the owner of the central temple also has additional temples elsewhere. Because he owns all of them, the congregation of each one is naturally connected to the others.

In Model IV, there are three sets of temples (A1A4, A2A3, A2A6, and A5A7, A5A8) and an independent temple (A9). To influence all the temples, one needs to contact the independent temple and the central church in each set (A1, A2, and A5); $x=4$.

The fourth model presents a situation where the central temple is connected to satellite temples owned by individuals who have been trained through the same patriarch-priest. They remain *pitit-kay*

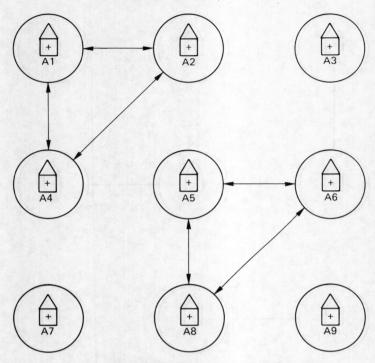

3   Model III: Temples with Common Ownership

(devotees), and their congregations are an extension of the central temple. Their associate temples continue to request the help of the patriarch-priest whenever they need it.

In Model V, there are two independent temples (A3, A9) and two sets of temples (A1A4, A4A2, and A5A6, A5A8, A8A7). To influence all the temples, one needs to contact the two independent churches and the central unit in each set (A4 and A5); $x=4$.

The fifth model is the situation where the central temple has its associates who have in turn their own associates. The second row of associates have received their training from the first associates, who have received theirs from the central temple. In other words, these satellite centres may also generate relations with dependent churches without losing their ties with the central church. They play a central role in relation to the satellite churches and a satellite role in relation to the central church.

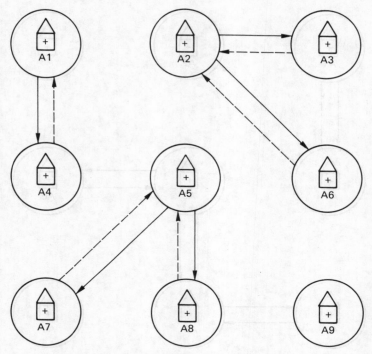

4   Model IV: Temples with Asymmetrical Relationships

It is postulated here that the flow of communication goes from the central church to the periphery and *vice versa*. By co-opting the central figure, it is possible to have access to his congregation, the associate-priests and the congregations of his associates. However, there is no guarantee that all associates in the network will follow the political will of the central figure, although his moral authority may make it a little easier to convince others.

In the beginning of the Duvalier era, Voodoo priests who were members of the opposition did not enjoy the same privilege as pro-Duvalier priests who resented maintaining their affiliation with opposition temples because they could be said to be dealing with enemies of the regime. As a result, the pro-Duvalier priests put pressure on each participating church in the network to support Duvalier so that they could operate in relative security.

The political exploitation of the Voodoo priests by the Duvalier

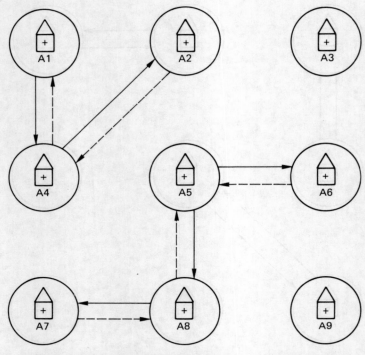

5   Model V: Temples with Satellite and Subsatellite Relationships

regime was accomplished through the use of an ideological ritual. For example, Duvalier arranged to make his public announcements on the 22nd of the month because 22 was known to be the Duvalier family's lucky number.[6]

One of the aspects that has been overlooked in the analysis of the interplay between Voodoo and politics is the political use of Voodoo secret societies (Laguerre 1980b: 147–160). My research in Upper Belair indicates that the secret societies are a paramilitary group connected to the Voodoo temples and that the most powerful bands of Mardi Gras and Rara are owned and operated by the leadership of the secret societies. The co-optation of these local leaders as Tontons Macoutes deeply grounded the political regime in the populace. For example, during the carnival season, these bands used political songs in which they portrayed François Duvalier as a good papa, a benefactor of the new Haiti. Also, these bands were allowed to circulate in the streets of Port-au-Prince on the eve of 22 May to show popular support for the administration of Jean-Claude Duvalier.

The Voodooisation of Haitian politics is partly due to the fact that there are individual politicians who have become Voodoo practitioners to protect themselves from the malevolent intent of others – in fact, Voodoo accusation is part of Haitian daily political life. The rumour that a prominent politician uses Voodoo to ensure his success is likely to make an opponent seek help from Voodoo. In my judgment, several politicians have become Voodooists precisely because they seek political office – a sharp contrast to the majority of the Haitian masses who practise Voodoo because they are ill or have illness in the family.

François Duvalier made no attempt to make the Voodoo church into a state church; to do so would have given fuel to his critics because he maintained that he was not a Voodooist. He also understood the possible international implications of such a move. Nor did it seem to have been part of his cultural renaissance programme. For their part, neither have Voodoo people exerted any sustained pressure on either François or Jean-Claude Duvalier to change their status.

THE POLITICISATION OF HAITIAN VOODOO

Political brokers, whether they function at the national or local level, tend to exploit the system to their own advantage because of their strategic position. This means that political dependency is not uni-directional. While the Voodoo church depends on the national elite for recognition, the elite are also dependent on Voodoo people for support. The politicisation of Voodoo basically means the recognition of the Voodoo church as a centre of power in the local community and of the Voodoo priest as a broker on behalf of his congregation.

The politicisation of Voodoo goes hand in hand with the political status of the Voodoo priest. At times, it has been a question of survival for the church (Deren 1953: 160). From the Haitian Revolution onwards the Voodoo temple has been used to plot political manoeuvers and the Voodoo priest has participated along with his congregation in creating political turmoil (Laguerre 1974a). To understand the politicisation of Haitian Voodoo during the Duvalier era one must focus on the Voodoo priest's status as a local politician, the identification of the Voodoo temple as a Duvalierist institution, and the incorporation of the late François Duvalier in the pantheon of Voodoo spirits.

Before the Duvalier era, the Voodoo priest was from time to time incorporated into the national political structure by astute politicians to combat or advance a specific cause (Rigaud 1953). Their presence was needed and their help sought for the success of ephemeral revolts in the mid-nineteenth century or even during the US occupation. Until 1950, Voodoo priests played a minor role in the election of the head of state because the president was elected by the Haitian congress and not by popular vote. However, they were more active during the period that preceded the end of an administration. Strikes by university students and the business community were always backed up by the proletariat of Port-au-Prince, most of them connected with a Voodoo temple and some of them members of secret societies. And once an administration had been pushed out of office, Voodoo priests were the first to parade and dance in the streets of Port-au-Prince and organise nightly *peristyle* (patio) parties for the residential community surrounding their Voodoo temples to celebrate their victory.

The Voodoo priest's political role can be appreciated when one understands how territorial and mystical space is divided in Haiti. Each priest or network of priests has control over a certain territorial domain granted to him because of his affiliation with a specific spirit or a central temple (Laguerre 1980a). This domain cannot be crossed over by another Voodoo group. That situation is made clearer when one looks at a Bizango passport, for example. On that passport are written the names of persons and villages who welcomed and honour it.

Duvalier used this network of Voodoo temples to control the residential communities that surround them – controlling one central temple gains one access to all the others. However, a satellite temple in a network may also have an autonomous stance on specific political issues. It is here that one may see the tension between the political options of the centre *vis-à-vis* those of the periphery. A local leader may decide for both personal and strategic reasons to further his own interests. More often, however, the priest in the central temple will influence those on the periphery.

During the administrations of both Duvaliers, many Voodoo priests joined the Tonton Macoute force for the following reasons: to be able to operate their temple freely without any harassment from the state, to maintain control over their own domain, to compete with neighbouring priests, to provide security for their own congregations, to serve as a broker with the government on behalf of their brethren, to become a prominent figure of authority in the community, to ensure a monthly salary from their job as a Tonton Macoute – or simply because they did not have any alternative.

Here we find a *modus vivendi* between the government and the Voodoo community and its priest. The government allowed the priest-Tonton Macoute to strengthen his leadership role and to practise his religion freely, but at the same time, the priest provided information on the community to the government – which gave the government an opportunity to maintain its grip on the neighbourhood. In this dialectical relationship, the Voodoo church became an extension of the government function in the community. There was here a symbiotic relationship between the government and the Voodoo church that helped maintain the ecological balance of power. This evidently rooted the regime very deeply in the local community.

Before François Duvalier became president, the Voodoo temple functioned mainly as a religious and medical centre. During his administration, one more ingredient was added to it. Political meetings were held there as well as ceremonies, intended to propagandise the regime. The *loas* were manipulated to speak in praise of the regime and extol its accomplishments. The spirits were also under government control. In Port-au-Prince, the terms 'Tonton Macoute' and 'Voodoo priest' became synonymous in some districts. It was almost impossible for one to be an influential Voodoo priest without being a Tonton Macoute or for a Voodoo church to be successful without being headed by a priest-Tonton Macoute.

As a result, the temple became the place where people sometimes came to seek help, not necessarily from the Voodoo priest as priest but from the priest as Tonton Macoute. If he happened to be the most influential Tonton Macoute in the district, his influence extended well beyond his congregation. Non-Voodooists as well as Voodooists came to see him and depended on him for protection against police and Tonton Macoute brutality.

The politicisation of the Voodoo church went beyond the priest's participation in national and local level politics, it penetrated the internal structure of the Voodoo ritual itself. The Duvalierist flag was used when the priest presided over a ceremony. It was also common to see the priest carry a Tonton Macoute revolver on his waist while invoking a spirit and to see other Tontons Macoutes in uniform performing with him. The most profound penetration of national politics in the church was through the canonisation of François Duvalier who is now venerated as a Voodoo spirit.

In the summer of 1976, while I was attending a Voodoo ceremony in Upper Belair, I was suprised to see the priest dressed up to resemble François Duvalier – in a dark suit and black hat, wearing heavy reading glasses and holding a pistol in his right hand. He spoke with a nasal voice, imitating François Duvalier's speech. I asked another Voodoo priest who was sitting next to me to identify the spirit for me. He replied that he was '*loa 22 os*.' I later found out that, in the Voodoo pantheon, François Duvalier is known as *loa 22 os*. The magical number 22 that he had so often used during his administration seems to follow him even after his death.

The canonisation of a government official as a Voodoo spirit is not new in the political history of Voodoo (Rigaud 1953). Throughout the history of Haiti, political leaders have been canonised and venerated as Voodoo spirits.[7] For example, Toussaint Louverture and Jean Jacques Dessalines figure prominently in the pantheon of Voodoo spirits (Duvalier 1968a: 178). For the Voodooists, Duvalier is one such national political hero.

CONCLUSION

The Duvalier administration's contribution to our understanding of the structural organisation of the Voodoo church is invaluable. By systematically co-opting the Voodoo priests, it has brought the Voodoo church openly into the political process and enabled us to see a series of linkages and ramifications from the nucleisation of Voodoo temples.

A Voodoo priest may exert some influence on other priests' political behaviour and is often part of a network of contacts. In fact, the urban Voodoo centres with which I am familiar maintain links with peripheral temples. These contacts may or may not be frequent. For example, the rural priest may visit his urban homologue in search of a new cure or may send a patient to him. Rural centres are sometimes an extension of an urban centre. In addition, there are in certain Voodoo centres other Voodoo priests who do not own a temple but serve as associates. Thus, a Voodoo priest in Port-au-Prince can influence other priests' decisions, and a clever politician may not have to deal with Voodoo priests on a one-to-one basis, but can rather enlist the help of the most influential ones, as Duvalier did.

One element that became evident in the Duvalierisation of the Haitian Voodoo church was that some temples emerged as nuclei of a network, not as isolated although autonomous units. Although the Voodoo church is not as hierarchically centralised as the Catholic church, most Voodoo churches are part of a network.

Voodoo church leaders who do not belong to the same temple tend to compete among themselves. A politician can exploit their weaknesses by co-opting them so as to control their organisation. By elevating the status of the Voodoo priest to that of a Tonton Macoute and by enabling them to operate in the open rather than underground the government could better monitor their activities and exploit them politically.

One must recognise here the ability of the François Duvalier administration – not necessarily the president himself, but his entourage – to circulate Voodoo-related gossip in the local communities. This served to enhance the regime's power. In a country like Haiti, what is important is not the veracity of these stories but whether they effectively project a certain image and perception of the government.

Two exogenous factors also made possible the Duvalier dynasty's manipulation of the Voodoo church. The regime's sympathy toward Voodoo was eased by the insistence of the Second Council of the Vatican for tolerance of local religious customs and the desire of the elite for a slow 'Haitianisation' of the local Catholic church. Without this social context, the Duvalierisation of the Voodoo church would have met more resistance from the larger Catholic community.

The Duvalierisation of Voodoo made the church more acceptable to a large segment of Haitian society – before François Duvalier's administration people were ashamed to speak of their Voodoo affiliation. During the administrations of both Duvaliers, even the bourgeoisie gave Voodoo names to their children as a form of cultural renaissance.

A mutation in the political use of Voodoo occurred from François to Jean-Claude Duvalier. François Duvalier ruled the masses through the use of local centres of power, among them the Voodoo churches. Jean-Claude Duvalier went one step further by integrating these centres into the rural development process. The Voodoo priests and their cohorts were also members of local community councils. Sometimes they played a leadership role within these structures or at least motivated their flock to join this governmental effort (Laguerre 1976b). They evidently continued to use their church as a power base.

One of the major consequences of the Duvalierisation of Voodoo is that it is a force to be reckoned with in the post-Duvalier era. The Voodoo church will continue to be a power base in the local community, and the Voodoo priest will maintain his role of broker or middleman to enhance his prestige, power and popularity. Thus, every constitutional president of Haiti will need a functional knowledge of Voodoo if he wishes to become a popular and successful leader.

This analysis of Voodoo and politics confirms the idea that religion can be used in a functional way to politically dominate a sector of society and, in return, that religious leaders can serve as political brokers. It allows us to understand a multiplicity of arrangements of the local churches and their links to the central political system. It also tells us that, in a situation of asymmetrical relationships, both poles are able to take advantage of each other, even though one definitely has the upper hand. Here is an instance where religious ideology was recuperated by the mainstream political system and used strategically to maintain a system of domination and inequality.

8 Public Policies and National Prospects

The analysis of the relationship between Voodoo and politics reveals the ramifications of Voodoo in both local and national level politics throughout the history of Haiti. During the colonial era, the slave and maroon leaders used the church to give impetus to the liberation movement that was crucial in their attempt to overthrow the colonial regime; more recently, the Duvalier administrations co-opted church leaders in an effort to control their organisation and the surrounding neighbourhood communities they served. If one may argue that Haitian politicians have always exploited the church to their advantage, it is also accurate to say that Voodoo has used in its hierarchical and regional organisation the imagery of the administrative structure of the Haitian governmental system. This is why I consider it important to look at how the state's politico-military structure is reflected in the church's organisation. Here is one focal point whereby the intersection between Voodoo and politics can be fruitfully analysed.

Voodoo today uses various political and military titles that are similar to those that have been used by either the military or civilian government ever since the colonial period – although the government was no longer using some of the titles when the status of the nation changed from kingdom to republic. Voodooists have continued to use them in their church. Once a government title is appropriated by Voodoo it tends to remain functional longer there than in the secular structure of the state – the linguistic categories in Voodoo are more culturally resilient than similar ones found in government. For example, the title of queen does not correspond to any governmental function in Haiti today, but it is still used in the hierarchical structure of the Voodoo church. Although government titles are used in the context of a specific form of administration, Voodoo, in contrast, tends to accumulate both old and new political and military titles. For example, one finds next to the president in the Voodoo church a queen, even when the leader is not using the title king. However, not all past and present government titles are used in Voodoo – some are and others are not.

The early description of Voodoo provided by Moreau de Saint-

Méry (1958) points to the existence of a king and a queen as the two leaders of the local church. No doubt this was a remnant of past African practices. Although the existence of the king of France was known by some slaves, he was not considered to be a high priest – a title that African kings held. If during the colonial period the title of Voodoo king was derived from a recent African past, after independence, a syncretism of functions occurred, probably due to the Voodooists' exposure to the reality of the kingdom of Henri Christophe (King of Haiti, 1807–1820). As the old slaves died, the referents to the king's secular functions were likely to be Haitian ones, but those to the king's religious functions were probably still mythic African king figures. This interpretation is based on the fact that the king of Haiti was never the religious head of a particular church so he was not a religious leader but, like the king of France, a political leader with religious responsibilities. Following the change in the political status of the country from kingdom to republic there was also a change in the title, though not necessarily in the functions, of the Voodoo priest from king to president. Even today, the high priest of a Voodoo temple may hold both a political function – as head of a secret society – and a religious one, as head of a church.

Identification of the head of government as a religious leader is not unique to Voodoo. In Palestine, we find Jesus referring to himself as a king or as the lord. For that matter, an entire doctoral dissertation has been written on the political, religious and biblical titles of Jesus (Sabourin 1961). There is even today a Sunday set apart in the Catholic church to celebrate the believed reality of Jesus the King.

Political and military symbolism can be found in the ritual itself, the division of the Voodoo territory, the titles of the spirits and the hierarchy of the church. It is my contention that the history of the Haitian people can also be unveiled through decoding the political and military symbolism of the Voodoo church.

THE GOVERNMENT OF GOD

Since the colonial era, Voodooists have developed their own theological view of the supernatural world, which they see in terms of a complex politico-military structure that operates on a spiritual as well as a human level. The major spirits are known to have a specific function in this government, and each one has a military or political title. For example, General Clermeil is believed to be in charge of

springs and rivers, General Brisé is supposed to protect the trees of
Chardette, Baron Samedi is a senator and diplomat. Zaka is minister
of agriculture and Loko is minister of public health while Danbala is
minister of finance. Agoué is a navy officer, the highest ranking
member of the Coast Guards. *Loa 22 os*, a Voodoo spirit embodying
François Papa Doc Duvalier, is president for life. Ogou is a brigadier
general, Sobo is a captain of the armed forces, Jean Baptiste is a
lieutenant general. Carrefour is president (Herskovits 1971: 228).
Legba is minister of the interior. In Baron Cimetière, one finds the
Haitian imperial title of 'Baron' – there are several spirits in the
Guédé family who hold that title.

In this government, as well as in any military or civilian one, there
is a compilation of titles and functions and one does not necessarily
contradict the other. It is important to note here that there was an
adaptation of roles in the case of the ancestral African spirits, that
is, they continued in Haiti the functions they had performed in Africa.
In the case of the Creole spirits, they tend to hold the same functions
they had while living on earth. For example, Jean Jacques Dessalines,
the first emperor of independent Haiti, is now a Voodoo spirit called
Empereur Dessalines – he is an emperor in the government of God.

The Voodoo clergy have also borrowed titles and functions from
the civilian government.[1] During the colonial era, the priest was
known as the king of the group; now he has the title of president.
He receives all the honours of a head of state from other Voodooists,
and he has an army of both spirits and men to protect the territory
under his supervision. One finds also a *honsi* with the function and
title of Queen Silence (*Reine Silence*). The *ogénikon* is known as
Reine Chanterelle (Singing Queen). Probably the most common title
in any Voodoo society is the *'Laplas'*. This is a post-colonial
government title, a contraction that stands for *'Commandant de la
Place'*. In the nineteenth century politico-administrative vocabulary,
he was the military head of a region and, the government's official
representative. The same titles one finds among the spirits are acted
out by Voodooists when they are possessed. For example, when
Baron Samedi possesses an individual, his 'host' dresses up like a
diplomat.

The site of the ritual provides a niche where the politico-military
symbolism of Voodoo can be decoded. The temple is the place where
ritual, mystical and territorial spaces meet and where territorial
divisions are structurally reduced under the same roof. The large
territory under the charge of the priest and the regional territory

under the command of the *Laplas* are here physically and symbolically represented. In other words, inside the temple, the political functions of the state are represented in the persons of various degree holders. Territorial and administrative distances between the priest (president); and the *Laplas* (military head of a region) are reduced and coalesced in the same ritual site. The territorial divisions that make up the political geography of Voodoo are represented by the spirits (or those who are possessed by them), whose respective domain of governance is the sea, the crossroad, the forest, the cemetery and so on.

The paraphernalia used in the temple probably best symbolises the military imagery in Voodoo. The flag is that of the 'society,' which is an army unit. The machete used by the *Laplas* represents the sabre used in the nineteenth century by the *Commandant de la Place*. Ogou's stick represents the rifle used during the post-independence era by the *général de Division* or the brigadier General. They symbolise the strength of the government of God to vanquish all enemies.

Spirits and degree holders occupy functions similar to those found in the various forms the Haitian government has experienced: empire, kingdom, presidency for life, military junta, council of government, term presidency and the various branches of government including the executive, the judiciary, the legislative and the army. Voodoo provides us in a very compact way with the political history of Haiti – which can be decoded through an analysis of titles used in the church. We find layers of historical sequences compacted in the titles and paraphernalia used by Voodooists within the realm of their church.

VOODOO SPACE

Before one can start looking into the policy options of the state, one must have an idea of the territorial organisation of the Voodoo church. The appropriation of territorial space by the Voodooists is an indication of the peripheral political status of the Voodoo church. However, one must distinguish between ritual, mystical and territorial space. Ritual space can easily be localised, is known by both Voodooists and non-Voodooists, and can serve a private or a public function. As a public space, it can be used by the congregation as well as by the public. As a private space, it can be used only by the spirits, the priest, his assistants, and Voodooists who are invited to do so.

Voodooists construct their mystical space through mental mapping. It is seen as a sacred space with its topography and the places where the spirits live. This mystical space encompasses both ritual and territorial space.

Unlike the Catholic church or state church, whose dioceses coincide with departmental boundaries, Voodoo territorial space intersects but does not coincide with the departmental divisions of the territory.[2] It comprises a set of spatial units that may intersect with one another and that are under the mystical control of Voodoo spirits, the religious control of one or more priests and the military control of a secret society.

PUBLIC POLICY

Throughout the history of Haiti, the state has developed five different strategies to deal officially with Voodoo: (1) outlaw it, (2) physically persecute it, (3) ignore it, (4) recognise it as genuine national folklore and (5) politically exploit the church. None of these policies – or the lack of them – has dealt in any appropriate manner with the issue.[3] I think that we now understand the parameters of the church and are better informed about its structural features to develop a policy that, on the one hand, recognises and protects the civil rights of the Voodoo practitioners and, on the other, reflects the general sentiment of the nation.

The Voodoo church has always been outlawed in Haiti, a policy inherited from the French colonial regime. President Jean Pierre Boyer officially outlawed the church in his rural code, although this policy was more to embellish the image of the country abroad than to forcefully eradicate or uproot the church. President Salomon, who was himself a Voodoo believer and who used to consult a Voodoo priestess named Reine Ti Bonne (Jean 1938: 30), had opted to officially ignore it. President Vincent outlawed the church and persecuted it with the help of the Catholic church. President François Duvalier – who had the means to officially recognise the church – did not do so. However, he invited Voodoo priests to participate in his government and allowed them to practise Voodoo openly.

State policies *vis-à-vis* the church have never been appropriate because they have not been based on an understanding of the issue but were, instead, responses to external and internal pressures. The views of Voodoo people have never been sought and consequently they have never upheld the state's negative policies toward their church.

Historically, church persecution has always been felt where the secret societies are not well organised. In the Artibonite *Département*, where they have an underground network of cells, they have been able to protect their temples and memberships – this may explain why the Voodoo church is stronger there than in the south, for example.

Before one can hope to understand church organisation and how its functioning relates to state policies, two epistemological questions need to be clarified. First, one must distinguish the church from its paramilitary organisations – the secret societies – and this is where the 'problem' lies. Second, it is unrealistic to believe that there is a Voodoo 'problem' in Haiti or that the state can eliminate the church. Voodoo is not a problem, but a reaction to unremitting national problems. Voodoo has developed its paramilitary organisations to 'save' the independence of Haiti. Even today they still remain in the eyes of rural folk a main avenue for the preservation of national security against any foreign invasions. They provide safeguards against the appropriation of peasant land by military officers, prominent politicians and the bourgeoisie. They provide the kind of justice that they believe the state cannot provide. Until these problems are solved the secret societies will continue to function as an underground police force and judicial body, although their judicial codes and moral values do not coincide with those of the state. Evidently one is dealing here with a dual system of government: one above ground and one underground. What is the way out of this dilemma? Our goal here is only to clarify some aspects of the issue and not necessarily to provide a set of recommendations.

There are in Voodoo two separate organisations that one must distinguish from each other: one is the church, and the other is the paramilitary government with its judicial body, its army and its network of spies. The church performs its ceremony in the open, and its membership is known to the public. The secret society is an underground organisation, and like all secret organisations, its membership, rules and policies cannot be revealed to outsiders. The church fills a religious, medical and recreational function in the neighbourhood, while the secret society has mainly a judicial and police function.

If the state decides to give official recognition or status to the Voodoo church, the latter has to be structurally separated from the secret society. Although there may be good ideological reasons to propose that Voodoo be made a church with a legal right to existence, the same cannot be said of secret societies – unless they were to change their *modus operandi*. However, they will not fade away until the state is able to provide the following safeguards to the Voodooists that the secret societies provide: protection of their land against spoliators, protection from rival Voodoo groups, protection of the community against outsiders' abuses and punishment of citizens who violate the law and general moral rules of the community. One cannot eliminate the secret societies as an underground organisation without also eliminating the reasons for their existence.

The state may want to continue to exercise surveillance over the secret societies because they hold the potential to engage in illegal or unlawful activities. Their organisations must be registered with the state: permission must be required if they want to continue to hold evening marches. Of course, to curtail possible fights and retaliation among members of competing groups, these evening rallies must be under state control and the local police must be able to protect those on whom the secret societies prey. Furthermore, they should not be allowed to pass judgement in their underground courts, not even in cases of witchcraft accusation. Finally, people should be encouraged to report without fear for their lives any unlawful activities or threats by members of secret societies.

Official recognition of Voodoo could be beneficial to both state and church. It may lead the Voodoo church to participate in the ecumenical dialogue with the other churches. It may also either trivialise the church by eliminating the shroud of mystery that surrounds it or eventually transform it into a competitive political institution. At the same time, it will allow the state to know more about the day-to-day activities of the Voodoo church. Because the Voodoo church is also a provider of medicine, its medical practices must be under state surveillance: the Voodoo priest currently practises medicine without a licence.

However, official recognition of the church may not necessarily solve the dilemma because there is no guarantee that the church can be separated from the secret societies. For that to happen, the state must be able to provide the local communities with the previously listed protective measures. If the state fails, regional branches of the existing secret societies will probably proliferate. This could eventually lead to chaos and internecine wars and weaken the regular army's ability to protect the citizens of the republic.

So far, effective persecution of the secret societies has been carried out by the US marines, the Catholic and Protestant clergy and zealous members of those churches – but not by the army. In an interview with a soldier-informant in a village on the central plateau, I found to my surprise that the majority of the armed forces there – who serve basically as a police force – hold membership in the Bizango secret society. I was told that this is a common practice throughout the country because at night the soldiers are forced to patrol alone the streets of the village or the city where they reside. They join the secret societies out of fear because they believe that their lives would otherwise be endangered. Furthermore, some members of the army are too dependent on Voodoo for promotion and are much too afraid of the malevolent intent of Voodooist fellow officers to engage in any aggressive activities against these secret organisations. By and large, the army has so far been unable to protect the peasantry against the nightly and sometimes unlawful activities of the secret societies. Since the independence of Haiti in 1804 the peasantry has not yet experienced one single evening without a curfew or a night during which they could circulate freely inside or outside their hamlets or villages without having to carry a secret society's passport in their pockets or purses for protection. The state must liberate peasants from this kind of burden of fear and interference in their private lives.

The Voodoo question is an issue of national importance, for after the fall of the dynastic Duvalier regime many Voodoo priests were killed and their temples destroyed. This is the second time in less than 50 years that their churches have been vandalised and they have been physically abused. Disagreement with the practices of Voodoo is not a valid reason for the persecution of practitioners. Although Voodooists are numerically a majority, they hold a minority status as a religious group. There is an urgent need, I believe, to seek a solution to this dilemma. However, there are so many aspects in regard to the development of appropriate state policies toward Voodoo in Haiti that it seems legitimate for the government to create a commission with the task of further studying the question and providing applicable recommendations.

Notes and References

1 Religion and Politics

1. One can think more particularly of the Voodoo stories reported by Newell (1888), Alaux (1856), and St John (1884). During the US occupation, several books with a sensationalist character were written on Voodoo. Among the most popular were Seabrook (1929), Craige (1934), and Wirkus and Taney (1931).
2. Caribbean colonial societies are often referred to in the literature as 'slave societies' (Goveia, 1965), 'slave plantation societies' (Hall, 1971), 'colonial societies' (Balandier, 1966), 'plantation societies' (Wagley, 1971), and 'Creole societies' (Brathwaite, 1971).
3. Baron de Wimpffen (1911, p. 27), who visited Haiti for the first time in 1788, noted that most of the colonists were not there to stay. Similarly, in his *Lois et Constitutions*, Moreau de Saint-Méry (1785, I: 11) spoke of the common habit among the colonists to say that they were going back to Paris the following year. According to Vaissière (1909: 300), there were in 1752 39 sugar mills in the district of Léogane. The majority of them were run by managers, not by their owners. In the census of 1774, among the 5000 planters listed, 2000 were absentees (Hilliard D'Auberteuil 1776, II: 79).
4. According to the census of 1681 (Vaissière 1909: 21), there were 6658 persons: 4336 free people and 2322 slaves. The census of 1687 reported the black slave population at 3582 (Vaissière 1909: 21). After 1687, the slave population continued to increase yearly until 1791.
5. In 1701, there were more than 10 000 slaves in Léogane alone (Galliffet 1701); in 1708, there were 3264 in Cap-Français (Beaussire de la Grange 1708). In 1716, the black population was augmented by 4000 (Blénac and Mithon 1716); in 1720, by 3667 (Duclos 1721); and in 1753, by 5260 (Lalanne 1754). The census of 1753 (Vaissière 1909: 116) reports that there were 12 799 whites, 4732 freedmen, and 164 859 slaves. In the census of 1775, we find 20 438 whites, 5897 freedmen, and 261 471 slaves (Vaissière 1909: 116). From the information provided by Wimpffen (1911), Dantès Bellegarde (1953: 28), and Malenfant (1814: III), we can evaluate the population of Haiti in 1789 at 21 166 white men, 9660 white females, 10 000 free mulatto and black men, 26 000 free mulatto and black women, 15 000 mulatto slaves, 455 000 active black slaves, and 200 000 slave children and slaves over 45 years of age.
6. For further elaboration on the role of slave religious leaders in slave revolts, see Barrett (1974), Bastide (1971), and Simpson (1970).
7. State–church relations have never been static for any nation. The content of the relations may change over time. This is especially so for persecuted churches in the communist world (see Simon 1970), but it also applies to other settings. For the evolution of state–church relationships in Latin America, see the classic work by Mecham (1966).

129

8. For an elaboration on the history of state–Voodoo relationships in Haiti, see Métraux (1958), Courlander and Bastien (1966), and Robert (1965).

2   The Evolution of Colonial Voodoo

1. The best accounts of colonial Voodoo are provided by Descourtilz (1935), Moreau de Saint-Méry (1958), Dalmas (1814), Malenfant (1814), and Madiou (1922).
2. Deschamps (1960), Thomas *et al.* (1969), and Mbiti (1970) are very useful in helping one understand the ecological basis of West African religious traditions.
3. On slavery in colonial Haiti, see particularly Debien (1974) and Gisler (1965).
4. Although several writers, Métraux (1958), for example, point to the Dahomean origin of Haitian Voodoo, Montilus thinks otherwise. See his article in Haitian Creole published in Sel (Montilus 1978).
5. Even today the African spirits have the upper hand in Voodoo. The Creole spirits are auxiliary to the African ones (Laguerre 1980a).
6. For a discussion of the formation, evolution and functioning of slave medicine, see Laguerre (1987a).
7. In his PhD dissertation Sosis (1971) presents a balanced view of slave religion in colonial Haiti.
8. Estimates of the population vary from one author to another. The breakdown of the population by class adopted here is reported in Justin (1826: 144).
9. On the missionary work of religious orders among the slaves in colonial Haiti, see the following sources: Sosis (1971), Breathett (1961), D'Allanche (1904), Jan (1951), and Le Ruzic (1912).
10. The decree for the expulsion of the Jesuits from the colony is reported in Gisler (1965: 178–179).
11. See also Malenfant (1814), Drouin de Bercy (1814), and Descourtilz (1935).
12. On the colonial administration's policy toward Voodoo, see Vaissière (1909).
13. See particularly Babb (1954), Debien (1953), and Wright and Debien (1975).
14. On the role of slaves as catechists, see Fouchard (1972: 499), who, reports, referring to a decree of 18 February 1761, that 'Et comme les esclaves avaient pris l'habitude de se réunir à l'église de jour et de nuit, qu'ils avaient institué parmi eux des bedeaux et des marguilliers, que ces dignitaires passaient d'une maison ou d'une habitation à l'autre pour prêcher et catéchiser, qu'ils prêchaient même dans l'église en l'absence du prêtre: toutes ces manifestations leur furent interdites'.

3   Marronage and Voodoo

1. Probably the best known autobiography of a maroon is that of the Cuban Montejo (1968).

2. For an analysis of the phenomenon of urban marronage in Cuba, see Deschamps Chapeaux (1969).
3. Moreau de Saint-Méry (1958) provides bits and pieces of information for an analysis of the maroon political, economic and religious system.
4. Oral traditions among secret societies relate that, in the maroon camps, the chief often used a messenger to contact the chiefs of other bands. To my knowledge, the bulk of information on Haitian history is not to be found solely in history textbooks but also in the oral traditions of the common people.
5. On the issue of the Christianisation of the slaves, see Laguerre (1973a).

4 Revolutionary Voodoo Leaders

1. The whole question of slave religion is debated in Sosis (1971) and Laguerre (1973a) through analyses of primary archival materials. See Raboteau (1978) for the Deep South of the US.
2. Some historians attribute this essay to Lafond Ladebat, others to Barbé de Marbois and still others to Bellaud Varennes (see Price-Mars 1928: 142).
3. Mennesson-Rigaud (1958) has documented the role of Voodoo in the revolutionary wars for independence.

5 Secret Societies

1. Although it is not proper to publish *in extenso* a copy of the Bizango passport that an informant has allowed me to make a slide of, I may, however, present additional information here concerning its content. It is signed by a council of elders composed of nine individuals. The passport is addressed to God, Men, Saints, Ancestors, other secret societies, villages, hamlets and cities of Haiti. The name of the founder and place of residence is given, as well as that of the carrier. The founder in this case is a woman. This tells us that both men and women are founders of secret societies in Haiti.

    The secret word, which is repeated three times, is also written on the passport, as well as the password, which is a Latin formula borrowed from the rituals of the Catholic church. The secret word is probably from an African dialect. It does not seem to derive from Haitian Creole because I could not recognise it. The secret word identifies the national network of secret societies; the password identifies the local branch to which the passport's carrier belongs.

    Probably the most interesting things written on the passport are the names of the villages, cities, and hamlets. 34 of them appear as places where the passport is honoured. On the basis of this information, one may conclude that the Bizango society operates in six out of the nine *Départements* of Haiti.
2. Davis (1986) presents ethnographic data to support my sociological interpretation of the Bizango phenomenon in Haiti. For different views

on the issue, see Herskovits (1971), Hurston (1938), Courlander (1960), and Hurbon (1979b).

3. There are two main clues to indicate that secret societies are an outgrowth of the colonial maroon's experience. Moreau de Saint-Méry refers to a box containing a snake which believers used during the Voodoo ceremony. There may be a symbolic continuity between the colonial box and the coffin that the secret societies use today. The second clue is found in the passwords used by the slaves. Malenfant wrote, 'Il y avait à Gouraud une grande prêtresse du vaudou et un noir grand chef. J'ai su ce fait par une négresse qui était initiée. *Il y avait un mot de passe*, mais elle n'a jamais voulu me l'indiquer . . . *Elle m' a donné les signes pour la reconnaissance avec la main*: C'est à quelque chose près celui des maçons . . . Elle me le dit sous le secret, en m'assurant que . . . *Je serais tué ou empoisonné si Je cherchais à découvrir le grand mystère de la secte*' (cited in Fouchard 1972: 536). This text informs us about the existence of the password, the handshakes, and the admonition not to reveal the secret and the possible consequences if one does. (Author's italics.)

4. The Piquets direct association with Voodoo and indirect association with the secret societies was revealed in *Le Temps*. In the edition of 16 August, 1902, one reads, 'La chose qui nous interesse le plus, c'est la durée de cette nouvelle crise aiguë à la faveur de laquelle se réveillent tous les instincts sauvages des "piquets", *ces anarchistes noirs, sectateurs du culte africain, fétichiste et cannibalesque, du Vaudou*, dont les haines ataviques d'anciens esclaves inspirent ces placards menaçants pour les étrangers affichés sur les murs du Cap et dont les fureurs incendiaires viennent de réduire en cendres Petit-Goâve.' (Author's italics.)

6   Pilgrimage, Voodoo and Politics

1. Data for this chapter were gathered while I was in Saut D'Eau during the summers of 1962 and 1963. A field trip sponsored and financed by the University of Illinois Research Board allowed me to do further research on Saut D'Eau during the winter of 1974. I am grateful to the villagers and particularly to Rev. Freud Jean and M Victor Jean, two Saudolese, for the comments on an earlier French draft of this chapter. I am also grateful to Dr Jean Baptiste Romain, Dean of the Faculty of Ethnology of the State University of Haiti, to Dr Norman E. Whitten, Jr of the University of Illinois, and to the late Dr Vera Rubin of the Research Institute for the Study of Man for their encouragement to write this chapter.

2. On the use of the apparitions in Champs-de-Mars for Soulouque's political purposes, Justin Bouzon writes: 'Vers le commencement du mois de juillet 1849, sur une propriété du champs-de-Mars de Port-au-Prince, la crédulité publique, habilement exploitée, voyait des signes manifestes de faits miraculeux qui se produisaient sur un palmier dominant la place. La Sainte Vierge, ayant le divin enfant dans ses bras, faisait de fréquentes apparitions, mais elle ne se faisait voir qu'à des

élus. Un jour il fut permis à tout le monde de voir la Vierge. Une feuille sèche se détache de l'arbre et sur la tache qui en tomba, les plus incrédules pouvaient voir le portrait de la Mère de Dieu. On ramassa la feuille fort respectueusement et on l'apporta au palais. Un premier peintre appelé pour tracer les contours de l'image déclara ne rien distinguer; un second, un mystificateur, qui n'entendait nullement se mettre mal avec le Chef de l'Etat, en suivant les marques de l'eau imprimées sur la tache, montra les formes générales de la Vierge, destinées par la nature, puis le manteau et enfin une couronne formée sur la tête . . . Voilà comment le ciel lui-même avait destiné une couronne à Soulouque' (Cabon 1933: 406).

3. Haiti is divided into nine *départements*, 27 *arrondissements*, 118 *communes*, and 558 *sections rurales*. The *commune* is administered by a communal council (*Conseil Communal*), which is presided over by a mayor.

4. In July 1924, Emmanuel Jeannot published a short pamphlet containing useful information on the curative waters of Saut D'Eau.

5. Religion has always been strongly linked with and manipulated by politicians in Haiti. During the Haitian Revolution (1791–1803), ringleaders and maroons used Voodoo as a religious and political ideology to get rid of the French (Laguerre 1973a, 1974a, 1974b). Since independence in 1804, politicians have never neglected to have some prominent Voodooists on their side to maintain political control over the masses (Laguerre 1973b, 1976a, 1980a).

   Under the Duvalier regime, Voodoo ceremonies were under government control and Voodoo priest activities were watched over (Laguerre 1976b). The Catholic church itself is not free of government control. Since the concordat of 1860, archbishop and bishops, on the very day of their episcopal consecration, need to take an oath of faithfulness to the Haitian government. Church rectors need to have presidential approval to be appointed to their new functions. This is precisely to prevent the church from becoming a state within the state (Courlander and Bastien 1966).

7 Politics and Voodoo During the Duvalier Era

1. The Voodoo priest is not simply a religious or medicine man, he is also a political person. He is the locus of 'personal power' because he serves as a middleman between his congregation and the Voodoo spirits and of 'institutional power' because he is a mediator between the political establishment and his community. While in the former case he plays an intermediary role because of his religious power, in the latter he does so because of his influential position.

2. For a useful essay on the 'phenomenon of the appropriation of the cultural manifestations of certain social groups by others in society and their transformation into national symbols', see Oliven (1984).

3. A collection of Duvalier's writings on Voodoo was published in *Les Oeuvres Essentielles* (Duvalier 1968a). See also Laguerre (1982b).

4. Lorimer Denis and François Duvalier published studies of Voodoo rituals in 1938, 1939 and 1940 as they were establishing the foundations of the indigenous movement in Haiti.
5. For an account of the anti-Voodoo policy and practice of the Catholic Church, see Robert (1965).
6. For an explanation of the content of that ritual, see Laguerre (1982a: 106).
7. Duvalier (1968a: 178) wrote, 'Je tressaillis de stupéfaction quand, ce soir du 24 décembre au cours d'un service en l'honneur du tout-puissant Pétro, le dynamisme émotionnel parvenu à son paroxysme, la personnalité du houngan chavira dans l'hypnose et que surgit des profondeurs de sa conscience: Dessalines l'empérator. C'était vraiment lui, le visage farouche, la physionomie fanatique, et tout le corps sculpté en un geste de vengeur.'

8   Public Policies and National Prospects

1. Voodoo is not the only folk institution that borrows the titles of its dignitaries from the government, others have used the same strategy. For example Rara, Mardi Gras bands, secret societies, co-operative labour groups and so on are all organised hierarchically using government titles. Titles such as king, queen, president, general, minister and senator are employed in these Haitian folk institutions.
2. The secret societies are multi-departmental organisations and protect all the Voodoo temples and congregations under their aegis. The territorial division of Voodoo is made up of networks of sites, each network being under the surveillance of a secret society.
3. The following texts against the practice of Voodoo were issued by the Haitian government in the nineteenth and twentieth centuries. In Jean Pierre Boyer's *Pénal Code* of 1826, one reads: 'Art. 405. Tous faiseurs de ouangas, caprélatas, vaudoux, Donpèdre, macandals et autres Sortilèges seront punis de trois mois à six mois d'emprisonnement et d'une amende de soixante gourdes à cent cinquante par le tribunal de simple police; et en cas de récidive, d'un emprisonnement de six mois à deux ans et d'une amende de trois cents gourdes à mille gourdes, par le tribunal correctionel, sans préjudice des peines plus fortes qu'ils encourraient à raison des délits ou crimes par eux commis pour préparer ou accomplir leurs maléfices.

   Toutes danses et autres pratiques quelconques qui seront de nature à entretenir dans la population l'esprit de fétichisme et de superstition seront considérées comme sortilèges et punies des mêmes peines.

   Art. 406. Les gens qui font métier de dire la bonne aventure ou de deviner ou de pronostiquer, d'expliquer les songes ou de tirer les cartes seront punis d'un emprisonnement de deux mois au moins et de six mois au plus et d'une amende de cent gourdes à cinq cents gourdes.

   Tous individus condamnés pour les délits prévus au présent article et en l'article 405 subiront leur peine dans les prisons maritimes et seront employés aux travaux de la marine.

Ils seront, en outre, à l'expiation de leur peine, placés sous la surveillance de la haute police de l'Etat, pendant deux ans, par le fait seul de leur condamnation.

Art. 407. Les instruments, ustensiles et costumes servant ou destinés à servir aux faits prévus aux deux articles précédents seront de plus saisis et confisqués, pour être brulés et détruits' (cited in Simpson 1970: 254).

In the article 12 of Président Riché's *Loi sur la Police des Campagnes*, one reads 'Tous les individus condamnés par un tribunal compétent pour sortilèges, tels que vaudou, macandats, dompèdres, ouanga, tires-de-cartes, etc. subiront leurs peines dans les prisons maritimes et seront occupés aux travaux de la marine' (cited in Montilus 1972: 299).

President Geffrard in the 'Circulaire No. 4034 Aux Commandants D'Arrondissement' ordered them to act 'avec fermeté à faire disparaître de notre sol ces derniers vestiges de l'esclavage et de la barbarie et à remplacer ces pratiques superstitieuses par le culte du vrai Dieu' (cited in Montilus 1972: 300).

On 5 September, 1935, during President Stenio Vincent's term in office, a decree against the practice of Voodoo was issued: 'Art. 1. Sont considérés comme pratiques superstitieuses: 1) les cérémonies, rites, danses et réunions au cours desquels se pratiquent en offrande à des prétendues divinités, des sacrifices de bétail ou de volailles; 2) le fait d'exploiter le public en faisant accroire, par des moyens occultes, qu'il est possible d'arriver soit à changer la situation de fortune d'un individu, soit à le guérir d'un mal quelconque, par des procédés ignorés de la science médicale; 3) le fait d'avoir en sa demeure des objets cabalistiques servant à exploiter la crédulité ou la naïveté du public.

Art. 2. Tout individu, convaincu des dites pratiques superstitieuses, sera condamné à un emprisonnement de six mois et une amende de quatre cents gourdes, le tout à prononcer par le tribunal de simple police.

Art. 3. Dans les cas ci-dessus prévus, le jugement rendu sera exécutoire, nonobstant appel ou pourvoi en cassation.

Art. 4. Les objets ayant servi à la perpétuation de l'infraction prévue dans l'article 3 seront confisqués' (cited in Simpson 1970: 255).

Bibliography

Archival Materials

ARCHIVES DU MINISTÈRE DES COLONIES (PARIS)
Arrêté du Conseil de Léogane, 16 juin 1711. Archives des Colonies F3 269.
Archives des Colonies, 1777.
Archives des Colonies, 1783.
Estimation de la quantité de Nègres étant dans la Colonie en 1767. Archives du Ministère des Colonies, Correspondance Générale, 2e série, Carton XIX.
Dénombrement de Mai 1681. Archives du Ministère des Colonies, Correspondance Générale, vol. I.
Lettre de M de Galliffet, du 22 mars 1701. Archives du Ministère des Colonies, Correspondance Générale, vol. V.
Rapport de M de Beausire de la Grange, ingénieur. Archives du Ministère des Colonies, Correspondance Générale, vol. VIII, 1708.
Lettre de MM de Blénac et Mithon, du 15 juillet 1716. Archives du Ministère des Colonies, Correspondance Générale, vol. XII.
Lettre de M Duclos, du 15 mai 1721. Archives du Ministère des Colonies, Correspondance Générale, 2e série, Carton VII.
Lettre de M de Lalanne, du 27 mars 1754. Archives du Ministère des Colonies, Correspondance Générale, vol. CXV.
Lettre de M de Montarcher, du 8 mars 1772. Archives du Ministère des Colonies, Correspondance Générale, vol. CXLII.
Lettre de MM de la Luzerne et de Barbé de Marbois, du 27 juillet 1787. Archives du Ministère des Colonies, Correspondance Générale, vol. CLVII.
Lettre de M D'Estaing au Ministre du Cap-Français, le 8 janvier 1766. Archives du Ministère de Colonies, Correspondance Générale, Saint-Domingue, C⁹ vol. CXXVII.
Lettre d'un habitant au Comte de Langeron, du 7 juin 1763. Archives du Ministère des Colonies, Correspondance Générale, Saint-Domingue, C⁹ vol. CXV.
Lettre de M LeNormand de Mézy, ordonnateur et sub-délégué de l'Intendant du Cap, du 16 janvier 1742. Archives du Ministère des Colonies, Correspondance Générale, C⁹ vol. VIII.
Lettre de M Laporte Lalanne, du Port-au-Prince, du 22 décembre 1757. Archives du Ministère des Colonies, Correspondance Générale, Saint-Domingue, C⁹ vol. C.
Lettre de Dubois de Lamothe. Archives du Ministère des Colonies, Correspondance Générale, Saint-Domingue, C⁹ vol. LXIX, 1751.
Lettre de MM Dubois de Lamothe et de Lalanne du Port-au-Prince, 25 octobre 1752. Archives du Ministère des Colonies, Correspondance Générale, Saint-Domingue, vol. CXX.
Mémoire de la Chambre d'agriculture du Port-au-Prince, 23 septembre 1764. Archives des Colonies C⁹ b 15.

Mémoire sur la colonie de Saint-Domingue, Archives des Colonies C³⁵ 28.
Mémoire sur les Nègres Marrons de Saint Domingue. Archives du Ministère des Colonies, Correspondance Générale, Saint-Domingue C⁹, 2e série, Carton XXXIII.
Mémoire sur la création d'un corps de gens de couleur levé à Saint Domingue, 1779. Archives du Ministère des Colonies. Correspondance Générale, Saint-Domingue C⁹, 2e série, Carton XXIX.
Moreau de Saint-Méry: Notes Historiques sur Saint Domingue. Archives du Ministère des Colonies, F³.
Quartier de Nippes, 29 août 1764. Archives des Colonies C⁹ B 16.
Règlement du Conseil du Cap, 1739. Archives des Colonies C⁹ B¹¹.
Règlement du Conseil de Léogane, Archives des Colonies, 1739.
Résumé balancé des Recensements de 1787 et 1788. Archives du Ministère des Colonies, Correspondance Générale, vol. CLX.
Supplique des Habitants du Fort-Dauphin, Rapportée dans l'Ordonnance Locale du 4 avril 1758. Archives des Colonies F³ 272.

ARCHIVES NATIONALES (PARIS)
Lettre des Pères Jésuites aux Administrateurs de Saint-Domingue, le 25/7/1708. Archives Nationales: Colonies B. 31.
Mémoire sur les Marrons. Papiers La Ferronaye, s.d. 1778? Archives Nationales T. 210³, 54è, Lions.
Mémoire aux Administrateurs de Saint Domingue du 1/1/1764. Archives Nationales: Colonies F³ 71.
Le Règlement de Discipline pour les Nègres adressé aux Curés des îles françaises de l'Amérique. Archives Nationales: Colonies F³ 90.

ARCHIVES DU PETIT SÉMINAIRE COLLÈGE SAINT-MARTIAL (PORT-AU-PRINCE)
Arrêt du Conseil Supérieur du Cap-Français, Ile de Saint-Domingue, qui condamne la morale et la doctrine des soi-disant Jésuites, du 13 décembre 1762. Archives du Collège Saint-Martial. 16 pages.
Gazette de Saint-Domingue, 14 mars 1764.
Relation d'une Conspiration tramée par les Nègres dans l'Ile de Saint Domingue; défense que fait le jésuite confesseur aux Nègres qu'on suppliciait de révéler les fauteurs et complices, 24 juin 1758 (s.l.n.d.) 8 pages.

Printed Materials

ADAMS, JAMES LEWIS (1970) *The Growing Church Lobby in Washington.* Grand Rapids: Eerdmans.
ALAUX, GUSTAVE D' (1856) *L'Empereur Solouque et Son Empire.* Paris: Michel Levy Frères.
APTHEKER, HERBERT (1968) *A Documentary History of the Negro People in the United States.* New York: Citadel Press.
ARRÊTÉ DU PRÉSIDENT D'HAÏTI du 26 janvier 1911, *Le Moniteur*, 28 janvier 1911.
AUBIN, EUGÈNE (1910) *En Haïti. Planteurs D'Autrefois, Nègres D'Aujourd'hui.* Paris: Armand Colin.

BABB, WINSTON CHANDLER (1954) *French Refugees From Saint Domingue to the Southern United States, 1791–1810*. PhD dissertation, University of Virginia.

BALANDIER, GEORGE (1966) The Colonial Situation: A Theoretical Approach. In *Social Change*, edited by I. Wallerstein. New York: John Wiley.

BARRETT, LEONARD E. (1974) *Soul-Force: African Heritage in Afro-American Religion*. New York: Anchor.

BASTIDE, ROGER (1961) *Les Religions Africaines au Brésil: Vers une Sociologie des Interpénétrations de Civilisations*. Paris: Presses Universitaires de France.

—— (1967) *Les Amériques Noires, les Civilisations Africaines dans le Nouveau Monde*. Paris: Payot.

—— (1970) *Le Prochain et le Lointain*. Paris: Cujas.

—— (1971) *African Civilization in the New World*. New York: Harper and Row.

BASTIEN, RÉMY (1966) Vodoun and Politics in Haiti. In *Religion and Politics in Haiti*, edited by Harold Courlander and Rémy Bastien. Washington, DC: Institute for Cross-Cultural Research, pp. 39–68.

BELLEGARDE, DANTÈS (1953) *Histoire du Peuple Haïtien, 1942–1952*. Paris: Imprimerie J de Gigord.

BEST, LLOYD (1968) Outlines of a Model of Pure Plantation Economy. *Social and Economic Studies* 17(3): 283–326.

BINCHY, D. A. (1941) *Church and State in Fascist Italy*. London: Oxford University Press.

BLET, PIERRE (1972) *Les Assemblées du Clergé et Louis XIV de 1670 à 1693*. Roma: Universita Gregoriana.

BRATHWAITE, EDWARD (1971) *The Development of Creole Society in Jamaica 1770–1820*. London: Clarendon Press.

BREATHETT, GEORGE (1961) The Jesuits in Colonial Haiti. *Historian*, February: 153–71.

BREMER, FREDRIKA (1868) *The Homes of the New World: Impressions of America*. New York: Harper and Row, 2 vols.

CABON, ADOLPHE (1933) *Notes Sur L'Histoire Religieuse d'Haïti. De La Révolution au Concordat* (1789–1860). Port-au-Prince: Petit Séminaire Collège Saint-Martial.

CHARLEVOIX, PIERRE FRANÇOIS-XAVIER DE (1730) *Histoire de l'Île Espagnole ou de Saint Domingue. Ecrite Particulièrement sur des Mémoires Manuscrits du P. Jean Baptiste Le Pers, Jésuite, Missionnaire à Saint Domingue, et Sur les Pièces Originales Qui Se Conservent au Dépôt de la Marine*. Paris: Hippolyte Louis Guérin, 4 vols.

CHARLIER, ETIENNE D. (1954) *Aperçu sur la Formation Historique de la Nation Haïtienne*. Port-au-Prince. Presses Libres.

CLARK, J., W. DENDY and J. PHILLIPPO (1865) *The Voice of Jubilee: A Narrative of the Baptist Mission, Jamaica*. London.

CONQUEST, ROBERT (1968) *Religion in the USSR*. New York: Praeger.

COURLANDER, HAROLD (1960) *The Drum and the Hoe*. Berkeley and Los Angeles: University of California Press.

COURLANDER, HAROLD, and RÉMY BASTIEN (1966) *Religion and Politics in Haiti*. Washington, DC: Institute for Cross-Cultural Research.

CRAIGE, JOHN HOUSTON (1934) *Cannibal Cousins*. New York: Minton, Balch.

D'ALLANCHE, DANIEL (1904) Les Missions des Capucins Français dans les Antilles au XVIIe Siècle. *Etudes Franciscaines* 12: 163–74.

DALMAS, ANTOINE (1814) *Histoire de la Révolution de Saint Domingue*. Paris: Mame Frères.

DAVIS, KINGSLEY, and MOORE, WILBERT E. (1945) Some Principles of Stratification. *American Sociological Review* 10: 242–9.

DAVIS, WADE (1986) *The Serpent and the Rainbow*. New York: Simon Schuster.

DEBBASH, Y. (1961) Le Marronage: Essai Sur la Désertion de l'Esclave Antillais. *L'Année Sociologique* 3: 1–112, 117–95.

DEBIEN, GABRIEL (1953) Colons de Saint-Domingue Réfugiés à Cuba (1793–1815) *La Revista de indias* 13(54): 559–605.

DEBIEN, GABRIEL (1966) Le Marronage aux Antilles Françaises au XVIIIe Siècle. *Caribbean Studies* 6(3): 3–43.

—— (1967) La Christianization des Esclaves aux Antilles Françaises au XVIIe Siècle. *Revue d'Histoire de l'Amérique Française* 20(4): 525–55.

—— (1974) *Les Esclaves aux Antilles Françaises (17ème et 18ème siècles)*. Fort-de-France: Société d'Histoire de la Martinique.

DENIS, LORIMER, and DUVALIER, FRANÇOIS (1938) Une Cérémonie du Culte Pétro. *Griots* 2(2): 156–9.

—— (1939) Une Cérémonie en l'Honneur de Damballah. *Griots* 3(3): 316–19.

—— (1940) Une Cérémonie d'Initiation: Le Laver Tête Dans le Culte Vodouesque. *Griots* 4(4): 657–9.

—— (1944) L'Evolution Stadiale du Vodou, *Bulletin du Bureau d'Ethnologie* 2(12): 1–29.

—— (1955) La Culture Populaire de la Poésie, du Chant et des Danses Dans L'Esthétique Vodouesque. *Bulletin du Bureau d'Ethnologie* 2(12): 1–29.

DEREN, MAYA (1953) *Divine Horsemen. The Living Gods of Haiti*. New York: Thames and Hudson.

DESCHAMPS, H. (1960) *Les Religions de l'Afrique Noire*. Paris.

DESCHAMPS CHAPEAUX, PEDRO (1969) Cimarrones Urbanos. *Revista de la Biblioteca Nacional Jose Marti* 2: 145–64.

DESCOURTILZ, MICHEL ETIENNE (1935) *Voyage D'Un Naturaliste en Haïti*. Paris: Librairie Plon.

DÉSIL, HÉROLD CLOTHES (1967) *Une Esquisse Ethnosociologique de la Communauté de ville-Bonheur Considérée dans Ses Rapports avec Certains Phénomènes D'Ordre Religieux*. Thèse de Licence. Faculté d'Ethnologie, Université d'Etat D'Haïti.

DE VAUX, ROLAND (1965) *Ancient Israel*. New York: McGraw-Hill.

DIEDERICH, BERNARD, and BURT, AL (1969) *Papa Doc: The Truth About Haiti Today*. New York: McGraw-Hill.

DROUIN DE BERCY (1814) *De Saint-Domingue, de Ses Ressources*. Paris: Hocquet.

DURKHEIM, EMILE (1915) *The Elementary Forms of the Religious Life*. London: Allen and Unwin.

DUTERTRE, JEAN-BAPTISTE (1667) *Histoire Générale des Antilles Habitées Par des Français*. Paris: T. Jolly, 4 vols.

DUVALIER, FRANÇOIS (1967) *Bréviaire d'Une Révolution, 40 Ans de Doctrine, 10 Ans de Révolution.* Port-au-Prince: Imprimerie de L'Etat.
—— (1968a) *Oeuvres Essentielles. Eléments d'Une Doctrine.* Port-au-Prince: Presses Nationales d'Haïti, vol. 1.
—— (1968b) *Oeuvres Essentielles. La Marche à la Présidence.* Port-au-Prince: Presses Nationales d'Haïti, vol. 2.
—— (1969) *Mémoire d'Un Leader du Tiers-Monde. Mes Négociations avec le Saint Siège ou Une Tranche D'Histoire.* Paris: Hachette.
EDMONSON, MUNRO S. (1960) Nativism, Syncretism and Anthropological Science. In *Nativism and Syncretism*, Middle American Research Institute, vol. 19. New Orleans: Tulane University.
FAHD, TONFIC (1973) Le Pèlerinage à la Mekke. In *Les Pèlerinages. De L'Antiquité Biblique et Classique à l'Occident Médiéval.* Paris: Geuthner.
FIELD, M. J. (1937) *Religion and Medicine of the Ga People.* London: Faber and Faber.
FOUCHARD, JEAN (1953) *Les Marrons du Syllabaire.* Port-au-Prince: Edition Henry Deschamps.
—— (1972) *Les Marrons de la Liberté.* Paris: Editions de L'Ecole.
FRASER, LIONEL M. (1896) *History of Trinidad, from 1781 to 1813.* Port-of-Spain: Government Printing Office.
GALTUNG, JOHAN (1972) A Structural Theory of Imperialism. *Journal of Peace Research* 2(3): 81–117.
GISLER, ANTOINE (1965) *L'Esclavage aux Antilles Françaises (XVIIᵉ–XIXᵉ siècle).* Fribourg: Editions Universitaires.
GOTTLIEB, ERIC (1970) Chalma Pilgrimage Pattern. PhD dissertation, Columbia University.
GOVEIA, ELSA V. (1965) *Slave Society in the British Leeward Islands at the End of the Eighteenth Century.* New Haven: Yale University Press.
GROSS, DANIEL R. (1971) Ritual and Conformity. A religious Pilgrimage to North Eastern Brazil. *Ethnology* 10(2): 129–48.
HAITI LITTÉRAIRE ET SOCIALE. Revue Bimensuelle de Port-au-Prince, 13, 20 juillet 1905.
HALL, GWENDOLYN MIDLO (1971) *Social Control in Slave Plantation Societies: A Comparison of Santo Domingo and Cuba.* Baltimore: Johns Hopkins University Press.
HERSKOVITS, M. J. (1971) *Life in a Haitian Valley.* New York: Anchor.
HILL, ROBERT B. (1971) *The Strengths of Black Families.* New York: National Urban League.
HILLIARD D'AUBERTEUIL (1776) *Considérations Sur l'Etat Présent de la Colonie Française de Saint Domingue.* Paris: Chez Grange.
HOBSBAWM, E. J. (1959) *Primitive Rebels: Studies in Archaic Forms of Social Movements in the 19th and 20th Centuries.* Manchester, Eng.: University Press.
HOUTART, FRANÇOIS (1977) Religion et Champ Politique: Cadre Théorique Pour l'étude des Sociétés Capitalistes Périphériques. *Social Compass* 24(2–3): 265–72.
HURBON, LAËNNEC (1979a) *Culture et Dictature en Haïti: L'Imaginaire Sous Contrôle.* Paris: L'Harmattan.

—— (1979b) Sorcellerie et Pouvoir en Haiti. *Archives de Sciences Sociales des Religions* 48(1): 43–52.

HURSTON, ZORA NEALE (1938) *Tell My Horse*. Philadelphia: Lippincott.

INNOCENT, ANTOINE (1906) *Mimola ou l'Historique d'Une Cassette. Petit Tableau de Moeurs Locales*. Port-au-Prince: E. Malval.

JEAN, ALFRED (1938) *L'Election de Monsieur Louis Etienne Félicité Lysius Salomon à la Présidence de la République: Une Séance de Nuit, de L'Assemblée Nationale (23 Octobre 1879)*. Port-au-Prince: Imprimerie Nemours Télhomme.

JAHN, JANHEINZ (1958) *Muntu: An Outline of Neo-African Culture*. London: Faber and Faber.

JAMES, C. L. R. (1963) *The Black Jacobins*. New York; Vintage Books.

JAN, JEAN-MARIE (1951) *Les Congrégations Religieuses au Cap-Français, Saint-Domingue: 1681–1793*. Port-au-Prince: Henri Deschamps.

JEANNOT, EMMANUEL (1924) *Guide du Pèlerin, Contenant d'utiles Renseignements sur les Eaux Curatives et des Cantiques en L'Honneur de Notre Dame de Saut D'Eau*. Port-au-Prince: Imprimerie V. Pierre-Noël.

JOLIBOIS, GÉRARD (1970a) Notre Principal Pèlerinage Marial. *Le Nouveau Monde*, no 1288, jeudi 30 juillet 1970.

—— (1970b) Notre Premier Pèlerinage Marial. *Le Nouveau Monde*, no. 1290, 1ᵉʳ août 1970.

—— (1970c) Notre Pèlerinage Marial. *Le Nouveau Monde*, no. 1296, 8 août 1970.

—— (1970d) Notre Pèlerinage Marial. *Le Nouveau Monde*, no. 1303, 18 août 1970.

JUSTIN, PLACIDE (1826) *Histoire Politique et Statistique de l'île d'Haïti*. Paris: Brières.

KERSUZAN, FRANÇOIS-MARIE (1896) *Conférence Populaire sur le Vaudoux Donnée par Monseigneur L'Evêque du Cap-Haitien*. Port-au-Prince: Imprimerie H. Amblard.

—— (1898) *Allocution Synodale de Monseigneur L'Evêque du Cap-Haitien . . . Sur la Nécessité Sociale d'Observer les Commandements de Dieu, et Allocution à la Réunion contre le Vaudoux le même Jour*. Cap-Haïtien: Imprimerie du Progrès.

KRIEGER, H. W. (1930) Aborigines of Ancient Island of Hispaniola. *Smithsonian Institution Report, 1929*: 473–506.

LABAT, JEAN BAPTISTE (1742) *Nouveau Voyage aux Iles de l'Amérique*. Paris: G. Cavalier, 6 vols.

LABORIE, P. J. (1798) *The Coffee-Planter of Saint-Domingue*. London: T. Cadelland.

LAGUERRE, MICHEL S. (1969) Le Sous-Développement Latino Américain. *Perspectives Sociales* 24(5): 130–4.

—— (1970) Brassages Ethniques et Emergence de la Culture Haïtienne. *Laurentian University Review* 3(2): 48–65.

—— (1973a) Nativism in Haiti: The Politics of Voodoo. Master's thesis, Roosevelt University.

—— (1973b) The Place in Voodoo in the Social Structure of Haiti. *Caribbean Quarterly* 19(3): 36–50.

—— (1974a) Voodoo as Religious and Political Ideology. *Freeing the Spirit* 3(1): 23–8.

—— (1974b) An Ecological Approach to Voodoo. *Freeing the Spirit* 3(1): 3–12.

—— (1976a) Belair, Port-au-Prince: From Slave and Maroon Settlement to Contemporary Black Ghetto. In *Afro-American Ethnohistory* in *Latin America and the Caribbean*, edited by Norman E. Whitten. Washington, DC: American Anthropological Association, Latin American Anthropology Group, pp. 26–38.

—— (1976b) The Black Ghetto as an Internal Colony: Socio Economic Adaptation of a Haitian Urban Community. PhD dissertation, University of Illinois.

—— (1976c) *Organisation Structurelle des Conseils Communautaires en Haïti.* Port-au-Prince: Inter American Institute of Agricultural Sciences of the Organization of American States (IICA/OAS).

—— (1980a) *Voodoo Heritage.* London: Sage Publications (Sage Library of Social Research, vol. 98).

—— (1980b) Bizango: A Voodoo Secret Society in Haiti. In *Secrecy: A Cross-Cultural Perspective*, edited by S. K. Tefft. New York: Human Sciences Press, pp. 147–160.

—— (1982a) *Urban Life in the Caribbean: A Study of a Haitian Urban Community.* Cambridge: Schenkman.

—— (1982b) *The Complete Haitiana. A Bibliographic Guide to the Scholarly Literature, 1900–1980.* Millwood, NY: Kraus International Publications, 2 vols.

—— (1986) Haitian Pilgrimage to Our Lady of Saut D'Eau. *Social Compass, International Review of Sociology of Religion* 23(1): 5–21.

—— (1987a) *Afro-Caribbean Folk Medicine. The Reproduction and Practice of Healing.* South Hadley, Mass.: Bergin and Garvey Publishers.

—— (1987b) *Electoral Politics in Haiti: A Public Opinion Poll.* Berkeley: Institute for the Study of Social Change, University of California at Berkeley.

LANTERNARI, VITTORIO (1963) *The Religions of the Oppressed.* New York: Knopf.

LÉGER, J. N. (1907) *Haiti, Her History and Her Detractors.* New York: Neale Publishing.

LE RUZIC, IGNACE-MARIE (1912) *Documents sur la Mission des Frères-Prêcheurs à Saint Domingue. Du Schisme au Concordat.* Lorient: Imprimerie Le Bayon-Roger.

LINTON, RALPH (1943) Nativistic Movements. *American Anthropologist* 45: 230–40.

MACKENZIE, N. I. (1967) *Secret Societies.* New York: Holt, Rinehart and Winston.

MACKLIN, JUNE (1973) Three North Mexican Golf Saint Movements. *Comparative Studies in Society and History* 15(1): 89–105.

MADIOU, THOMAS (1922) *Histoire d'Haïti.* Port-au-Prince: Imprimerie Chéraquit.

MAIR, LUCY (1959) Independent Religious Movements in Three Continents. *Comparative Studies in Society and History* 1: 113–36.

MALENFANT, COLONEL (1814) *Des Colonies et Particulièrement de Celle de Saint-Domingue: Mémoire Historique et Politique*. Paris: Audibert.

MANIGAT, LESLIE F. (1964) *Haiti of the Sixties, Object of International Concern: A Tentative Global Analysis of the Potentially Explosive Situation of a Crisis Country in the Caribbean*. Washington, DC: Washington Center of Foreign Policy Research.

—— (1977) The Relationship Between Marronage and Slave Revolts and Revolution in St Domingue, Haiti. In *Comparative Perspectives in Slavery in New World Plantation Societies*, edited by Vera Rubin and Arthur Tuden. New York: New York Academy of Sciences, pp. 420–38.

MARGAT, PÈRE (1827) Lettre due Père Margat, Missionnaire de la Compagnie de Jésus au Père . . . de la Même Compagnie, le 27 Février 1725. In *Lettres Edifiantes et Curieuses: Mémoires d'Amérique*. Paris: La Société Catholique des Bons Livres.

MARZAL, M. M. (1967) La Religiosité du Sous-Développement. *Parole et Mission* 39: 663–672.

MBITI, J. (1970) *African Religions and Philosophy*. New York: Anchor.

MECHAM, J. LLOYD (1966) *Church and State in Latin America*. Chapel Hill: University of North Carolina Press.

MENNESSON-RIGAUD, ODETTE (1958) Le Rôle du Vaudou dans L'Indépendance d'Haïti. *Présence Africaine* 17–18: 43–67.

MÉTRAUX, ALFRED (1957) *Haiti, La Terre, les Hommes et les Dieux*. Neuchatel: LaBaconnière.

—— (1958) *Le Vaudou Haïtien*. Paris: Gallimard.

—— (1972) *Voodoo in Haïti*. New York: Schocken.

MONTEJO, ESTEBAN (1968) *The Autobiography of a Runaway Slave*. Edited by Miguel Barney. New York: Random House

MONTILUS, GUÉRIN (1972) Haïti: Un Cas Témoin de la Vivacité des Religions Africaines en Amérique et Pourquoi. In *Les Religions Africaines Comme Source de Valeurs de Civilisation*. Paris: Présence Africaine, pp. 287–309.

—— (1978) Fini kont sa a: Vodou Ayisyin Soti Daomé. *Sel* 6(42): 28–33.

MOREAU DE SAINT-MÉRY, MÉDÉRIC LOUIS ELIE (1785) *Lois et Constitutions des Colonies Françaises de L'Amérique Sous le Vent, de 1550 à 1785*. Paris: Chez l'Auteur.

—— (1958) *Description Topographique, Physique, Civile, Politique, et Historique de La Partie Française de L'Ile de Saint-Domingue*. Paris: Société de L'Histoire des Colonies, 3 vols.

NAU, M., and TELHOMME, N. (1930) *Code Domanial 1804–1930*. Port-au-Prince: Maurice Telhomme.

NEWELL, WILLIAM W. (1888) Myths of Voodoo Worship and Child Sacrifice in Hayti. *Journal of American Folklore* 1: 16–30.

NICHOLLS, DAVID (1970) Religion and Politics in Haiti. *Canadian Journal of Political Science* 3(3): 400–14.

OLIVEN, RUBEN GEORGE (1984) The Production and Consumption of Culture in Brazil. *Latin American Perspectives* 11(1): 103–15.

OURSEL, RAYMOND (1963) *Les Pèlerins du Moyen Age*. Paris: Fayard.

PARRINDER, GEOFFREY (1970) *West African Religion*. New York: Barnes and Noble.

PARSONS, TALCOTT (1949) *Essays in Sociological Theory Pure and Applied*. Glencoe: Free Press.

PATTERSON, ORLANDO (1967) *The Sociology of Slavery*. Rutherford: Fairleigh Dickinson University Press.

PAUL, EMMANUEL C. (1962) *Panorama du Folklore Haïtien*. Port-au-Prince: Imprimerie de L'Etat.

PETERS, CARL EDWARD (1941) *Lumière Sur le Humfort*. Port-au-Prince: Imprimerie Chéraquit.

—— (1965) Société Mandinque. *Revue de la Faculté d'Ethnologie* 10: 48–50.

PEYTRAUD, LUCIEN (1897) *L'Esclavage aux Antilles Françaises Avant 1789*. Paris: Hachette.

PIERRE-CHARLES, GÉRARD (1967) *L'Economie Haïtienne et sa voie de Développement*. Paris: G.P. Maisonneuve et Larose.

—— (1973) *Radiographie d'Une Dictature. Haïti et Duvalier*. Montréal: Les Editions Nouvelle Optique.

PRICE-MARS, JEAN (1928) *Ainsi Parla l'Oncle*. Paris: Imprimerie de Compiègne.

RABOTEAU, ALBERT (1978) *Slave Religion*. New York: Oxford University Press.

RAINEY, FROELICH G. (1941) *Excavations in the Fort Liberté Region, Haiti*. Yale University Publications in Anthropology 23–4. New Haven: Yale University Press.

RAPHAËL, FREDDY (1973) Le Pèlerinage. Approche Sociologique. In *Les Pèlerinages. De L'Antiquité Biblique et Classique à l'Occident Médiéval*. Paris: Geuthner, pp. 11–30.

REDSONS, VICTOR (1970) *Genèse des Rapports Sociaux en Haïti*. Paris: Norman Béthune.

RIGAUD, MILO (1953) *La Tradition Vaudou et le Vaudou Haïtien*. Paris: Niclaus.

ROBERT, PAUL (1965) *L'Eglise et la Première République Noire*. Lampaul-Guimilliau: Centre Missionnaire St Jacques.

RODRIGUES, RAYMUNDO NINA (1932) *Os Africanos No. Brasil*. Sao Paulo: Companhia Editora Nacional.

ROTBERG, ROBERT I. (1976) Vodun and the Politics of Haiti. In *African Diaspora*, edited by Robert I. Rotberg. Cambridge: Harvard University Press, pp. 342–65.

ROUMAIN, JACQUES (1937) *A Propos de la Campagne Anti-Supersti-tieuse*. Port-au-Prince: Imprimerie de L'Etat.

ROUZIER, SÉMEXAN (1891) *Dictionnaire Géographique D'Haïti*. Paris: Charles Blot.

SABOURIN, LÉOPOLD (1961) *Les Noms et les titres de Jésus*. Paris: Desclée de Brouwer.

ST JOHN, SIR SPENCER (1884) *Hayti or the Black Republic*. London: Smith Elder.

SANNON, H. PAULÉUS (1920) *Histoire de Toussaint Louverture*. Port-au-Prince: Auguste A. Héraux.

SANTOS, THEOTONIO DOS (1968) *El Nuevo Caracter de la Dependencia*. Santiago: Cuadernos de Estudios Socio-Economicos 10, Centro de Estudios Economicos, Universidad de Chile.

SCHOELCHER, VICTOR (1842) *Colonies Etrangères et Haïti*. Paris: Pagrerre.
SEABROOK, WILLIAM B. (1929) *The Magic Island*. New York: Harcourt, Brace.
SHILS, E. (1974) *Essays in Center and Periphery in Macrosociology*. Chicago: University of Chicago Press.
SIMMEL, G. (1950) *The Sociology of Georg Simmel*. New York: Free Press.
SIMON, GERHARD (1970) *Church, State and Opposition in the USSR*. Berkeley and Los Angeles: University of California Press.
SIMPSON, G. E. (1970) *Religious Cults of the Caribbean: Trinidad, Jamaica and Haiti*. Puerto Rico: Institute of Caribbean Studies.
SOSIS, HOWARD JUSTIN (1971) The Colonial Environment and Religion in Haiti: An Introduction to the Black Slave Cults in Eighteenth Century, Saint-Domingue. PhD dissertation, Columbia University.
STREET, JOHN M. (1960) *Historical and Economic Geography of the Southwest Peninsula of Haiti*. Berkeley and Los Angeles: University of California Press.
LE TEMPS. Affaires d'Haiti 16 août 1902.
THOMAS, L. V., LUNEAU, B. and DONEAUX, J. (1969) *Les Religions D'Afrique Noire*. Paris: Fayard-Denoël.
TROUILLOT, HENOCK (1957) La Condition de la Femme de Couleur à Saint-Domingue. *Revue de la Société Haïtienne d'Histoire, de Géographie et de Géologie* 30(103): 21–54.
—— (1970) *Introduction à Une Histoire du Vodou*. Port-au-Prince: Imprimerie des Antilles.
TURNER, VICTOR (1974) *Dramas, Fields and Metaphors*. Ithaca: Cornell University Press.
TURNER, VICTOR, and TURNER, EDITH (1978) *Image and Pilgrimage in Christian Culture. Anthropological Perspectives*. New York: Columbia University Press.
VAISSIÈRE, GEORGE PIERRE CHARLES DE (1803) *Examen de l'Esclavage et Particulièrement de l'Esclavage des Nègres dans les Colonies d'Amérique*. Paris, 2 volumes.
—— (1909) *Saint-Domingue (1629–1789). La Société et la Vie Créole Sous L'Ancien Régime*. Paris: Perrin et cie.
VAN GENNEP, ARNOLD (1960) *The Rites of Passage*. Chicago: University of Chicago Press.
WAGLEY, CHARLES (1971) Plantation America: A Culture Sphere. In, *Caribbean Studies: A Symposium,* edited by Vera Rubin. Seattle: University of Washington Press.
WALLACE, ANTHONY F. (1956) Revitalization Movements. *American Anthropologist* 58: 264–81.
—— (1966) *Religion: An Anthropoligical View*. New York: Random House.
WEBER, MAX (1930) *The Protestant Ethic and the Spirit of Capitalism*. London: Allen and Unwin.
WEIL, THOMAS E., *et al.* (1973) *Area Handbook for Haiti*. Washington, DC: US Government Printing Office.
WILSON, B. R. (1973) *Magic and the Millennium: A Sociological Study of*

Religious Movements of Protest Among Tribal and Third World Peoples. London: Heinemann.

WIMPFFEN, BARON DE (1911) *Saint-Domingue à la Veille de la Révolution*. Paris: Louis Michaud.

WIRKUS, FAUSTIN, and TANEY, DUDLEY (1931) *The White King of La Gonâve*. New York: Doubleday.

WOLF, ERIC R. (1958) The Virgin of Guadalupe: A Mexican National Symbol. *Journal of American Folklore* 71: 34–39.

WRIGHT, PHILIP, and DEBIEN, GABRIEL (1975) Les Colons de Saint-Domingue Passés à la Jamaïque (1792–1835). *Bulletin de la Société d'Histoire de la Guadeloupe* 26(4): 1–267.

Index